FREEDOM, GLORIOUS FREEDOM

FREEDOM, GLORIOUS FREEDOM

THE SPIRITUAL JOURNEY TO THE FULLNESS OF LIFE FOR GAYS, LESBIANS, AND EVERYBODY ELSE

John J. McNeill

Beacon Press
Boston

Beacon Press
25 Beacon Street
Boston, Massachusetts 02108-2892

Beacon Press books
are published under the auspices of
the Unitarian Universalist Association
of Congregations.

99 98 97 96   8 7 6 5 4 3

Text design by John Kane
Composition by Wilsted & Taylor

Library of Congress Cataloging-in-Publication Data

McNeill, John J.
    Freedom, glorious freedom: the spiritual
journey to the fullness of life for gays, lesbians,
and everybody else / John J. McNeill.
        p.   cm.
    Includes bibliographical references.
    ISBN 0-8070-7936-7 (cloth)
    ISBN 0-8070-7937-5 (paper)
    1. Gays—Religious life.
2. Homosexuality—Religious aspects—
Christianity.   3. Twelve-step programs—
Religious aspects—Christianity.   I. Title.
BV4596.G38M65   1995
261.8'35766—dc20   94-15723
                                                        CIP

*Christ still sends me roses. We try to be formed
and held and kept by him, instead he offers us
freedom. And now when I try to know his will,
his kindness floods me, his great love overwhelms
me, and I hear him whisper, Surprise me!*
                  Ron Hansen, Mariette in Ecstasy

CONTENTS

ACKNOWLEDGMENTS

This book could never have been written without the support, encouragement, and assistance of my partner and lover of the last twenty-nine years, Charles Chiarelli. By his faithful and patient love, Charlie made me certain of what I say in this book through our own experience of gay love. He also worked alongside me for many years, preparing and proofreading manuscripts, patiently teaching me computer skills, and keeping me sane with his wry sense of humor.

I owe a special debt of gratitude to my sister, Sister Mary Sheila McNeill, for her continuous prayers and support for my ministry to gays and lesbians.

I also wish to thank Margaret and Larry Kornfeld, and Jack and Judy McMahon for their enthusiastic support, and for reading my manuscript and making many helpful suggestions.

All my retreatants at Kirkridge over the years deserve a special thanks for giving me valuable feedback as I developed the ideas in this book, with special gratitude to Robert Raines and Cynthia Hirni.

I wish to acknowledge also, all the wonderful lesbian and gay couples I have met over the years through various professional, spiritual, and personal events: Virginia and Debra, Philip and Dan, Joe and Duffey, Bill and Joe, Dick and Jerry, to mention only a few.

And last, and certainly not least, I wish to express special gratitude to Pat and Bruce for creating the *Chiron Rising* family and for giving us the opportunity to encounter so many genuine, loving gay couples including Denny and Mac, Dave and Bob, Bill and Tom, Bill and Dave, and many others.

P R E F A C E

While doing research for this book, I discovered that the Sanskrit root of the word for "freedom" has two interdependent meanings. First, it means to be a free (not a slave) member of the household of the master. Second, it means to be loved by the master. Anyone in the household that the master loved became a free member of the household because of that love. Anyone who was not loved was a slave member of that household.

I find the insight that comes from this double meaning of the word freedom very profound. It is love; it is knowing that we are loved; it is by living in an atmosphere of love that we humans are genuinely freed. The child that knows it is loved is free to play and to develop in a healthy way. We adults, if we are fully conscious of God's love for us, are psychically free to mature and to play life to its fullest in the presence of a loving God. Love creates the space in which freedom flourishes. It is this interrelationship between love and freedom that will be the primary focus of this book.

The title, *Freedom, Glorious Freedom*, is derived from a famous passage in the writings of Paul: "For the whole creation is waiting with eagerness for the children of God to be revealed. It was not for its own purposes that creation had frustration imposed on it, but for the purposes of him who imposed it—with the intention that the whole creation itself might be freed from its slavery to corruption and brought into the same glorious freedom as the children of God" (Rom. 8:19–21).[1]

Throughout my childhood I read that verse without comprehension. I did not feel free or loved because of my religious beliefs; I was raised in a religion of guilt, shame, and fear in relationship to a god of fear. It took a long process with the help of God's grace for me to liberate myself as a gay man from that god of fear and be able to discover on a personal level the God of love, revealed by Jesus. Now, thanks be to God, I can make this statement from Paul my own: "For what you received was not the spirit of slavery to bring you back into fear; you received the Spirit of adoption, enabling us to cry out, "'Abba, Father!' The Spirit himself joins with our spirit to bear witness that we are children of God" (Rom. 8:14–17). To be free, then, is to be aware that we are members of the household of a loving God.

This is the third book I have published on gay theology. In some sense the entire trilogy deals with freedom and liberation. The first book, *The Church and the Homosexual*, was a quest for intellectual freedom from the homophobic thought patterns of the past and a positive effort to arrive at an understanding of homosexuality as a gift from God, to be lived out and enjoyed. The second book, *Taking a Chance on God: Liberating Theology for Gays, Lesbians, and Their Lovers, Families, and Friends*, dealt more on the psychological level and was derived from my own personal struggle to free myself from all the wounds of homophobia in my psyche in order to live out my gayness with joy and gratitude.

This third book deals with the presence of the Spirit of God, the Spirit of love, in our daily experiences, and how, through communion with that Spirit, to arrive at the "glorious freedom" of the children of God. The first part of the book deals with freedom of conscience and discernment of spirits. These ancient teachings of the Christian church have a special urgency for lesbian and gay people who need to free themselves from all homophobic authorities and deal with God on a direct and personal basis. The second part deals with the liberating process of *coming out of the closet* seen as a spirit-filled effort to achieve the glory of God by becoming fully alive as gay people. The third part deals with twelve-step spirituality as a spiritual process of liberation from *all* addictions in order to experience the love of God in its fullness. The fourth part deals with the problems that gay people have in becoming aware of God's special love for them and also the unique qualities present in a gay person's love for God.

The focus is shifted in the epilogue. In this section, I am expressing a philosophical vision, looking both to the past and to the future, of how gay liberation fits into the Spirit-directed evolution of human history. This section is unavoidably intricate at times, so I ask the readers' patience and tolerance. I am convinced that such an overview of the teleological movement of the great dialectic in history is essential to a full understanding and acceptance of the role of gay liberation in history.

After more than twenty-five years of ministry with lesbian and gay persons, as both priest and psychotherapist, I am convinced that a unique spirituality, special and vibrant, is springing up in the gay community. It is a spirituality totally compatible with a life of gay sexual love and intimacy. As Scripture says, "the stone which the builders rejected has become the cornerstone" (Mark 12:10) on which God, with divine humor, builds the faith community. God's special presence to the gay community and the unique graces which are enabling gays and lesbians to build a vibrant and mature, autonomous spirituality are not just gifts meant for the gay community alone. When God pours out special blessings on one segment of the community, those blessings are meant to flow out and be shared by the human community at large. This is the reason for my subtitle: *The Spiritual Journey to the Fullness of Life for Gays, Lesbians, and Everybody Else.*

I frequently thank God that I was born in time for this historic period of gay and lesbian liberation. I am grateful to God also for the blessing and grace to have been able to be almost totally engaged in ministry to gay and lesbian Christians for this past quarter century.

The enormous response I have received over the past many years from lesbians and gay people who thank me and God for the grace of liberation they found in my books has been a clear witness to the fact that the Spirit of God has used me to bring true liberation and spiritual growth to hundreds, even thousands, of my gay brothers and sisters. I am truly grateful to God for being allowed to play that role. My prayer and my hope are that, with God's grace, this book will prove a source of liberation into holiness for all those who read it.

FREEDOM,
GLORIOUS
FREEDOM

PART 1

GAY SPIRITUAL
MATURITY

INTRODUCTION

The GAY SPIRITUAL JOURNEY

Recent insights developed in the field of psychology have undermined the traditional premises of the Catholic Church's teaching and pastoral practice concerning homosexuality. We now know that homosexuality is not just a question of indulgence in lustful behavior, as most Church documents obviously presuppose.[1] It is an orientation that is probably, at least in part, genetically determined. An orientation is a way of thinking, feeling, and responding that goes to a person's very essence. A gay orientation is not something that can be chosen. We are born gay! Our gayness is part of God's creative order. To claim, then, that homosexuality represents an "orientation to evil," or is the "result of original sin," as did recent Church documents, is to see God as cruel and sadistic. I

3

for one would much rather believe that the Church is wrong than that God is evil. ▼ Further, there is no scientific evidence that homosexuality is a changeable orientation. One can no more change one's sexual orientation than one can change the color of one's eyes from blue to brown. There is no way a gay person can become heterosexual. One can deny and repress one's gayness and undertake heterosexual behavior, but only at a great price both morally and psychologically. Those who attempt such conversions rely heavily on the cultivation of self-hatred and the worship of a god of fear. ▼ Since we gay people were born into an unchangeable gay orientation, we must live out that reality to the best of our ability. We have a desperate need to understand our lives and experience in a positive spiritual context. We need to hear the stories of others who have undertaken the gay spiritual journey with its unique perils and opportunities. ▼ It is my firm belief that the future of the Christian churches and a revitalized faith in the God of love lies not only in the base communities, the communities in Central and South America formed by the poor who attempt to discern from their own experience what God's will is for them, but also in the gay and lesbian faith groups here in North America and around the world. This is nothing new. Those familiar with gay and lesbian history are aware that spiritual leadership has always come in great part from the gay community in every culture and time. ▼ Anthropologists note that in many primitive cultures gays play a strong role in spiritual leadership. For example, in Native American tradition, the *berdache* or the *heyoehkah*, who gave spiritual leadership to the tribe, was usually drawn from its gay members.[2] Gays and lesbians have also played a leading, if hidden, role in Western monastic tradition. John

Boswell has documented that contribution, pointing out that
some of the most effective and saintly of monastic found-
ers, such as Saint Aelred of Rievaulx, were gay men.[3]
Granted that the homosexual or lesbian orientation is unchosen and unchangeable,
what should be the psychological
and spiritual path to psychic
and spiritual health for
lesbians and gays?

▼

CHAPTER 1

FREEDOM *of* CONSCIENCE
and GAY MATURITY

What Is Maturity?

A healthy maturing process is the process by which we separate off from our dependence on parents, family, and religious authorities and become autonomous adults, make our own choices, and take responsibility for them. Maturity is defined as the ability to live one's life according to one's own insights and feelings and no longer live in a continuous effort to meet the expectations of others. Theologian Sebastian Moore has even gone so far as to say that "living your life to meet the expectations of others" is a form of sin. On both the psychological and the spiritual levels, maturity means the ability to discern what is the true self and to find the courage to act out that true self.

In his book on the spiritual journey of the poor in the base communities of Central and South America, Gustavo Gutierrez, a Peruvian liberation theologian, expresses this same understanding of spiritual maturity. The title of his book *We Drink from Our Own Wells* derives from a famous saying of the medieval monk, Saint Bernard of Clairvaux: "Everyone has to drink from his [or her] own well." Spirituality, Gutierrez writes, is like living water that springs up from the very depths of our own personal spiritual experience.[1]

D. W. Winnicott, a famous English child psychologist, wrote: "Every child knows in its bones that in its wickedness lies hope; in its conformity and false socialization lies despair!"[2] Winnicott meant that most children remain hopeful that they will be loved and respected even when they do not conform to parental expectations. But if a child believes that the only way it will be loved is by conforming to the expectations of others and hiding the real self in a closet, it has already despaired of life. Many of the clients in my psychotherapy practice remember a secure, joyful childhood, which came to an abrupt end when they discovered that their spontaneous feminine self or, if they were lesbian, their spontaneous masculine self was totally unacceptable to their parents. The rest of their lives they spent an enormous amount of their psychic energy trying to suppress that unacceptable feminine or masculine dimension of the real self.

One of my clients shared with me his most intense childhood experience of shame. At a family get-together, he dressed up as a ballerina and, playing ballet music on the stereo, danced into the parlor expecting to entertain his family and receive their approval and admiration. He became, instead, painfully aware of his family's shock and revulsion. From that day on, he undertook a process of denying and suppressing everything feminine about himself. He became convinced that the feminine part of himself, which was an essential part of his real self, was somehow evil and unlovable—even to God. He cultivated a religion of fear to help him keep that feminine self repressed.

Maturity for a gay person must include coming out of the closet, just as spiritual maturity must include coming out of the closet with God. We must risk that we can be loved by God just as we are. We must "take a chance on God."

Freedom of Conscience

A central Christian teaching, going back to Jesus himself, is without doubt of utmost importance to lesbian and gay Christians. It is *freedom of conscience.* This teaching is based on Jesus' promise to his followers to send them the Holy Spirit who will dwell in their hearts.

At the Last Supper, Jesus promised: "I shall ask the Father and he will give you another Paraclete [the Greek word means "advocate"] to be with you for ever, the Spirit of truth whom the world can never accept since it neither sees nor knows him; but you know him" (John 14:16–17). Jesus further declared: "I have said these things to you while still with you; but the [Advocate], the Holy Spirit, whom the Father will send in my name, will teach you everything and remind you of all I have said to you" (John 14:25–26). The title "Advocate" which Jesus gives the Spirit means a "lawyer," one who speaks with us and for us, one who will plead our cause.

Paul, in his Epistle to the Hebrews, sees the gift of the Spirit as a fulfillment of this prophecy of Jeremiah:

> *Look, the days are coming, Yahweh declares, when I*
> *shall make a new covenant with the House of Israel*
> *when those days have come . . . . I shall plant my Law,*
> *writing it on their hearts. Then I shall be their God*
> *and they will be my people. There will be no further*
> *need for everyone to teach neighbour or brother, saying,*
> *"Learn to know Yahweh!" No, they will all know*
> *me, from the least to the greatest . . . since I shall*
> *forgive their guilt and never more call their sin to*
> *mind. (Jer. 31:31–34)*

Notice that Jeremiah foresees the new covenant where every human from the least to the greatest will have direct access to a God who dwells in their hearts. This access to God will not be the privilege of a few who are gifted with extraordinary intelligence, or ritual rank, or even holiness. The Holy Spirit is a thoroughgoing respecter of democratic process. There is no hint here that one must go to authorities in order to inform one's conscience; God directly and immediately informs our conscience, including those of gays and lesbians.

In the Acts of the Apostles on Pentecost Sunday, Peter recalls these words of the prophet Joel: "I shall pour out my Spirit on all humanity. Your sons and daughters shall prophesy, your young people shall see visions, your old people dream dreams. Even on the slaves, men and women, shall I pour out my Spirit" (Acts 2:17–18; Joel 3:1–2). Once again the emphasis is placed on the democratic nature of the Spirit.

At the Last Supper, Jesus informed his disciples that it was necessary that he should go away in order for the Spirit to come: "Yet you are sad at heart because I have told you this. Still, I am telling you the truth: it is for your own good that I am going, because unless I go, the [Advocate] will not come to you; but if I go, I will send him to you. . . . However, when the Spirit of truth comes he will lead you to the complete truth" (John 16:6–13). Why did this Spirit only come after Jesus' death? Because as long as Jesus remained alive and present, his disciples had their center of authority outside themselves and were not, therefore, totally responsible for their actions. They were striving to meet the expectations of someone else. They had not yet become fully creative and responsible adults. We have instances in the New Testament where Jesus sent his disciples out to preach and heal in his name, and then supervised how they performed, much as a supervisor would monitor a present-day social worker at the beginning of her or his career (e.g., Matt. 10:1–33).

But after Jesus' death his Spirit became what Paul saw as the source of the . . . *glorious freedom of the Children of God.* "The proof that you are sons [and daughters] is that God has sent the Spirit of his Son into our hearts: the Spirit that cries, '*Abba*, Father'; and it is this that makes you a son [or daughter], you are not a slave anymore" (Gal. 4:6–7). Paul clearly understood that the good news of the *Evangelium*, the gospel message, is exactly this message of our freedom: "Christ set us free, so that we should remain free. Stand firm, then, and do not let yourselves be fastened again to the yoke of slavery" (Gal. 5:1–2). Paul had the same understanding of freedom as found in the Sanskrit root of the word. The pagans are not free but slaves in relation to their gods because they relate to their gods in a spirit of fear. But Christians are free because their God is a God of love who has adopted them into his family. "All who are guided by the Spirit of God are sons [or daughters] of God; for what you received was not the spirit of slavery to bring you back into fear; you received the Spirit of adoption, enabling us to cry out, '*Abba*, Father!' The Spirit himself joins with our spirit to bear witness that we are children of God. And if we are children, then we are heirs, heirs of God . . ." (Rom. 8:14–17). Here again he expresses the theme of an escape from enslavement to the gods of fear: "But formerly when you did not know God, you were kept in slavery to things which are not really gods at all, whereas now that you have come to recognise God—or rather, be recognised by God—how can you now turn back again to those powerless and bankrupt elements whose slaves you now want to be all over again?" (Gal. 4:8–11).

Paul continually repeats the theme that God's Spirit dwells within us and, if we ask, will empower us: ". . . the Spirit too comes to help us in our weakness, for, when we do not know how to pray properly, then the Spirit personally makes our petitions for us in groans that cannot be put into words . . ." (Rom. 8:26). There is a yearning and a longing deep in our psyche which is not just that of our ego but that of the Spirit of God dwelling in the depths of our spirit. Maurice Blondel gives a philosophical expression to this same theme in his philosophy of action: "Our God dwells within us, and the only way to become one with our God is to become one with our authentic self."[3]

With the death of Jesus, then, and the coming of the Spirit, the apostles received a challenge as well as an opportunity to mature. As Paul expressed it: ". . . until we all reach unity in faith and knowledge of the Son of God and form the perfect Man, fully mature with the fullness of Christ himself" (Eph. 4:13). They had to give up the security of a provident leader; they had to find out what God wanted from them from within themselves and their own experience. It was only after the coming of the Spirit that the apostles found the courage to leave the security of their closet (the upper room) and go out into the world as responsible adult agents of the Spirit. In like manner, in our spiritual life, we gay people must pass from a passive, dependent role to an active, creative one. We have a special need to become mature, self-motivated, autonomous people, no longer passively dependent on outside homophobic sources for a sense of our identity and well-being. We must not let our enemies outside ourselves define us; we must let the Spirit of love that dwells within our hearts define us.

It is this understanding of the role of the Holy Spirit that gives me great consolation during those times when the Church reacts to its gay members in ignorance and even downright hostility. We gays should be thankful to God for creating a humanly fallible Church. We are intensely aware that if our parents had been infallible we could never have matured to become autonomous and responsible adults. We would spend our lives saying, "Yes, Mother," "Yes, Father." We would never develop our own capacity for independent judgment and, consequently, never feel personally responsible for our actions. God blessed us with finite and, consequently, fallible parents. It was precisely when and where our parents proved fallible that we were challenged to take distance from their authority, then make our own choices and be fully responsible for them.

In a similar way, we are dependent on the fallibility of religious authorities in order to develop an adult freedom of conscience. When we gays and lesbians discover that we cannot follow the fallible teachings of our religious authorities without destroying ourselves, then we are forced to search out what God is saying to us through our experience and take personal responsibility for the choices we make. I believe that the Holy Spirit is using the fallibility of the religious authorities to guide the Christian community into a new level of maturity and responsibility necessary for the spiritual growth of the human community in today's world.

CHAPTER 2

FREEDOM *of* CONSCIENCE *and*

the CATHOLIC CHURCH

The Catholic Church teaching on "freedom of conscience" was most recently restated in the conciliar documents of Vatican II:

> *Humans have in their hearts a law written by God. To obey it is the very dignity of the human; according to it we will be judged. Conscience is the most secret core and sanctuary of the human. There, we are alone with God, whose voice echoes in our depths. In a wonderful manner conscience reveals the law which is fulfilled by love of God and your fellow humans. In fidelity to conscience Christians are joined to the rest of humanity in the search for truth, and for the genuine solution to the numerous problems which arise from the life of the individual and from social relationships.* [1]

Conscience is described here as the voice of God speaking to us immediately from within our own consciousness of ourselves, without need of external mediation. A human's freedom to follow one's conscience is seen as the source of her or his true dignity. It was the inspiration of these words of the Vatican Council that led the gay Catholic organization at its first national meeting to choose the name "Dignity." This freedom is understood not as an anarchic principle but, on the contrary, as the only true foundation for real community and the only valid ground for a solution to social problems and relationships. According to this teaching, gays and lesbians also have direct access to the Spirit of God and God speaks to them directly in their experiences.

This doctrine of freedom of conscience is the best kept secret in the Catholic Church. Sometimes the hierarchy gives it a nod, only to vitiate it by maintaining that only an informed conscience is free and that it is their God-given right to be the sole informers.[2] With these words Pope John Paul II sets aside four decades of philosophical and theological work on how to put together respect for human autonomy and freedom with a corresponding respect for the law of God. Pope John Paul II is expressing an understanding of moral life as based on an objective rational reading of God's law revealed in nature. He is trying to remove all relativism and subjectivity from moral judgments and come up with absolute and definitive moral rules independent of human subjectivity and experience. The result is a repudiation of freedom of conscience and in its place a claim to an infallible authoritarianism (see appendix 3).

Every time the Church tries to exercise what is popularly referred to as "creeping infallibility" it tends to issue authoritative statements that are out of touch with the experience of the people of God. This is especially true in the area of sexual ethics. The hierarchy seems more concerned with preserving the authority of the institution than with promoting the true happiness and well-being, both psychological and spiritual, of the faithful. *Veritatis Splendor* is another example of this attitude. The result is that the faithful, following the guidance of the Spirit within, are "nonreceptive" of authoritative teaching.

The Church seems almost paranoid in its reaction to criticism. For example, it sees "manipulation" and "conspiracy" when Dignity asks for dialogue and a reexamination of the traditional teaching on homosexuality. Back in 1968 when the majority of experts on the Pope's Commission recommended qualified approval of artificial means of birth control, the Pope disbanded the commission and issued *Humanae Vitae*, reiterating traditional prohibitions. The result was an enormous drop in respect for and dependence on Church authority. Polls in 1993 show that 85 percent of married Catholics have made a decision in conscience to make use of artificial means of birth control in their sexual lives. As Bishop Francis Murphy of Baltimore points out: "In its discussion on the regulation of birth, the pastoral letter (*Humanae Vitae*) does not grapple with the important issue of the non-reception of the teaching of the magisterium."[3]

The reactionary stance of the Church hierarchy seems to imply that tradition is equivalent to God's will. There is no room for new insight or for the work of the Holy Spirit "leading us into all truth." For the hierarchy, God's will is manifested only from the top down, and the Church has no need to listen to what the Holy Spirit has to say in and through the lives of people who are attempting to live according to the Church's teaching.

According to the press, when Pope John Paul II made a recent visit to the United States, he came with over fifty prepared talks. He was so busy giving prepared speeches, usually scolding and critical in tone, he did not have a moment to listen. But why should he listen? As the Vatican likes to put it: There is no such thing as the American Church; there is only the Roman Church in America. So there is nothing for the Pope to learn from the unique quality of the Spirit's action in the Church in America.

Yet, I believe, there is something very unique about the American Catholic Church. It is perhaps the only Church in the world where a large percentage of the laity are so well-educated in theology, that they are, in fact, frequently better educated in their faith than are the clergy. When Cardinal O'Connor, for example, addresses a major theological issue, he sounds like an Irish-American politician. When, however, Governor Mario Cuomo addresses that same issue, he sounds like a well-trained theologian. While Catholic universities train laity to be critical thinkers, seminaries have rapidly become schools of indoctrination that discourage all thinking and suppress all dissent.

Archbishop Rembert Weakland observed that the glory of the Catholic Church in past ages was its willingness to enter into dialogue with the new insights of science and rethink its traditions in the light of these new insights. Today, the great challenge to all the churches is to rethink Christian traditions concerning sexuality in the light of new insights coming from psychology and sociology. Such a process has begun in the American Church (e.g., the recent Presbyterian and Lutheran reports on human sexuality) and has led to a readiness to reconsider women's roles in the Church and the meaning of homosexuality and a readiness to undertake new, more compassionate ministries to sexual minorities. It is precisely these new initiatives that the Vatican means to crush out and stigmatize.

What happened to the effort made by the American bishops to write, over a period of ten years, a pastoral letter addressing the issues of women in the Church, is a perfect example of the Vatican's suppression of new insights. The United States bishops began auspiciously by listening to women, some 75,000 of them, in 140 diocesan consultations. They consulted the experience of many whose talents and aspirations are unjustly overlooked, especially in the Church. The committee brought the listening process into the public domain and opened a dialogue that cannot be dismissed or ignored. This process raised awareness of women's concerns with the Church, not only in the United States, but in a number of countries around the world. The first draft of the pastoral letter clearly reflected the concerns of women and made several important steps toward recognizing their legitimate issues. For example, the letter called on the Church to acknowledge its sins of misogyny, seek God's forgiveness, and apologize to women. It also called for opening all positions of power in the Church to women and keeping open the debate on ordaining women to the priesthood. But then reactionary forces took over and, with the cooperation of Rome, rolled back the process so that every progressive insight was eliminated by the fourth draft. Bishop Murphy speaks of "the kind of harmful pressure being exerted by Rome on the legitimate process of discernment underway in the Catholic church in the United States . . ."[4]

The most serious objection that Vatican officials raised was their rejection of the consultation process used by the Committee on the Women's Pastoral. They asserted that "bishops are teachers, not learners; truth cannot emerge through consultation."[5] In many instances, the difficulties the committee ran into with Rome are identical to the problems the gay and lesbian community experiences in its effort to establish dialogue with the Church. In light of this impasse between the American

Church and Roman authority, we must reflect on the nature of the maturing process and the relation of a mature person to institutional authority.

Pathological Religion and Spiritual Maturity

Developmental psychology has made us very much aware of the gradual process by which the child separates off from the parent and achieves separate identity and relative autonomy. Dysfunctional families that make a pathological use of their authority can disrupt this process and undermine the maturing process for their children. The child needs the gradual failure of the parents to respond perfectly to its needs in order to grow up successfully, separate off, and become a mature, independent, autonomous human.

Contrary to psychological wisdom, the pre–Vatican II Church liked to pose as infallible, having the perfect answers to all questions. This overemphasis on authority can easily lead to "pathological" religion. Pathological religion has much in common with the dysfunctional family. It relies on fear of punishment to obtain obedience; it uses guilt as a subtle lever for manipulation and control. It fears freedom and cultivates blind, unquestioning obedience. Even normal doubts are punished and repressed because they are seen as threatening. As an illustration of a pathological interpretation of religious faith, consider this advertisement sponsored by the Knights of Columbus Religious Information Bureau. The advertisement appeared originally on October 24, 1965, in the *New York Herald Tribune* (this date was just before the end of the Second Vatican Council).

WHAT FAITH DOES
FOR THE CATHOLIC
MAN!

He sees in his religion, first of all, a means to the salvation of his immortal soul. But it also has a more immediate and urgent purpose—to teach him how to live!

The Catholic man does not have to invent his own theory as to the nature of God. He doesn't have to set

> *up his own code of ethics for his relations with other*
> *men. He doesn't have to formulate personal standards*
> *of moral and social behavior . . . or make his own*
> *distinctions between right and wrong, good and bad.*
>
> *All these problems are resolved for him by his belief*
> *in God's revealed truth . . . by the clear instructions*
> *found in the gospel of Jesus Christ . . . by his accep-*
> *tance of the Sacraments dispensed through the Church*
> *for the nourishment of his soul . . .*

The Catholic faith is identified here with total immaturity, passivity, blind faith, and obedience. Catholics are urged not to think or reflect or use any of our God-given skills. The Catholic depicted here is one who sees his or her duty as giving blind obedience to Church authority and not accepting responsibility for his or her actions. I like to refer to this kind of believer as the "Eichmann Christian." Karl Adolf Eichmann, who sent thousands of Jews to their deaths in the concentration camps, did so, he claimed, in good conscience because he was brought up to believe that his only responsibility was to be obedient to legitimate authority and never to question it.

Fortunately, the distortions of faith in this advertisement were corrected in many of the documents of Vatican II. For example, in the document *The Church in the Modern World*, issued in 1966, lay people are urged to accept their responsibility to apply Christian principles in the area of their expertise:

> *Laymen {persons} should also know that it is gener-*
> *ally the function of their well-formed Christian con-*
> *science to see that the divine law is inscribed in the life*
> *of the earthly city. From priests they may look for spir-*
> *itual light and nourishment. Let the lay person not*
> *imagine, however, that his {or her} pastors are always*
> *such experts that to every problem which arises, how-*
> *ever complicated, they can readily give him {or her} a*
> *concrete solution or that such is their mission. Rather,*
> *enlightened by Christian wisdom and giving close at-*
> *tention to the teaching authority of the Church, let the*

layman {person} take on his {or her} own distinctive role.[6]

According to this document the lay person's role is to be the mediator between the Church and the world, having the responsibility and corresponding right to determine how the message of the Gospel applies to the complicated problems in the field of his competence.

Vaclav Havel believes that the development of a free conscience will be essential for competent political leaders in the future:

> *Soul, individual spirituality, first-hand personal insight into things, the courage to be himself and go the way his conscience points, humility in the face of the mysterious order of being, confidence in its natural direction, and, above all, trust in his own subjectivity as his principal link with the subjectivity of the world—these are the qualities that politicians of the future should cultivate.*[7]

Many voices have been raised seeking a reform in the way authority is used in the Church. Among them is Sally Cunneen, a feminist theologian and seminary professor. In Cunneen's book *Mother Church: What the Experience of Women Is Teaching Her*, she explores the changes which would occur in the Church if it tried to live up to its ancient image as mother. She points out that the primary task of a good mother is not to dominate her children but to empower them: "The questions that a good mother asks and her ability to listen to the answers are themselves part of a mutual conversation of empowerment. The ability to hear the truth of a child's criticism at any age is essential to the mother's understanding and her growth in virtue."[8]

Cunneen sums up the pain as well as the value of such communication:

> *In the course of raising her children, the loving mother must allow for the possibility that her children will despise her. She must gradually disillusion them so that their idealization of her and their belief in her*

> *power and magic will disappear. Her children must*
> *finally see her as she is and come to recognize their own*
> *strengths. Surely this process of enduring feedback is*
> *essential to a Church that is . . . not only a holy*
> *mother but a church of sinners as well. She has need*
> *to hear the whole truth in order to disillusion her chil-*
> *dren about her perfection so that they might be better*
> *enabled to serve God in this world.*[9]

Another voice calling for "conversion" of the Church is Lad-islas Orsy, S.J., theologian and canonist. In his article "The Conversion of the Churches: Condition of Unity, A Roman Catholic Perspective" (*America*, May 30, 1992, p. 484), Orsy asserts that the essential condition for ecumenical unity among the churches would be a "conversion" of the Roman Church. That conversion would be a new recognition of the power of the Spirit in the laity:

> *Conversion can take on a very concrete meaning. It can*
> *mean a radical "turning to the people"—the recog-*
> *nition of the power of the Spirit in the laity, the ac-*
> *knowledgment of their sacred character, the granting*
> *to them of a greater share in the operations of the*
> *church. It ought to mean the establishment of insti-*
> *tutional structures guaranteeing that their concerns*
> *are listened and attended to by the hierarchy.*

Whenever the Church tries to exaggerate its authority and undermine the autonomy and individual responsibility of its members, then providentially, God lets it fall flat on its face. The result is that all of us see that "the emperor has no clothes" and we become personally responsible to discern spirits, exercise our freedom of conscience, make a personal choice, and accept full responsibility for that choice. We should thank God, then, every time we see evidence that God is granting the hierarchy in today's Church the grace of fallibility.

CHAPTER 3

DISCERNMENT *of* SPIRITS

Though the Church may fail us, each of us can have a direct and unmediated experience of the Spirit of God in our own personal life of prayer and contemplation, especially in our experience of mutual love. This personal experience is the only unpolluted water from which we gay people can drink. All messages mediated to us by our Church, our family, and our culture are for the most part polluted waters—polluted by homophobia. How do we gays go about "drinking from our own wells" in our spiritual life? By learning the ancient spiritual discipline called "discernment of spirits." God will speak to each of us directly through our experience, as long as we open ourselves and seek to learn God's will for us.

In this practice God speaks to us directly, not through our intellect, but primarily through our feelings. To *discern spirits* is to listen to our own hearts. Our God dwells within us and the only way to become one with our God is to become one with our authentic self. If any action we undertake brings with it deep feelings of peace, joy, and fulfillment, then we can be sure that what we are doing is right for us. To be able to discern spirits we must have made a total commitment of ourselves to God and be willing to do whatever God asks of us.

We gay and lesbian people should take heart from the example of Paul. He confronted the hierarchy of his Church on the question of submitting gentile converts to Jewish law, after he had made a personal discernment: "The question came up only because some . . . have furtively crept in to spy on the liberty we enjoy in Christ Jesus and want to reduce us all to slavery. I was so determined to safeguard for you the true meaning of the Good News, that I refused even out of deference to yield to such people for one moment" (Gal. 2:4–6).

On another occasion when Peter refused to eat with gentile converts because they did not follow Jewish dietary laws, Paul speaks of "opposing Peter to his face, since he was manifestly in the wrong" (Gal. 2:11–13). Obviously, Paul was able to trust not only his own experience but also what he heard God saying to him through his own discernment process—and he had the courage to act on those insights no matter what price he might pay!

In a modern-day courageous act of discernment, Bishop Francis Murphy of Baltimore has stated: "I am personally in favor of the ordination of women into a renewed priestly ministry. I believe this issue to be as important as the issue Paul raised with Peter, namely, the admission of Gentiles into Christianity. Women's calls, as well as men's, should be tested. Justice demands it. The pastoral needs of the church require it."[1]

Applying St. Ignatius' Discernment

With his extraordinary psychological genius, it was Ignatius of Loyola, the founder of the Society of Jesus, who drew up the "Rules for the Discernment of Spirits" as the central part of his Spiritual Exercises. Ignatius' practice of discernment began when he was carried home on a stretcher for a long convalescence after his legs were smashed by a cannon ball. He had only two books to read during his long weeks in bed. One was a life of Christ and the Saints, the other was a book of romantic tales. After reading the romances, Ignatius would daydream about winning the hearts of the women of the Court. Although he derived some pleasure from these daydreams of romantic conquest, he was aware that afterward he felt emptiness and sadness. However, after reading about the great Saints, he would daydream about outdoing them as a knight in the service of Jesus Christ. These dreams filled him with a sense of peace and joy that would last for a long time.[2]

Ignatius discerned from this that God was calling him into the service of Jesus. So, leaving his armor at the feet of the Virgin Mary in the monastery of Montserrat, he entered into a cave in Manresa and spent ten months in prayer. During those months, Ignatius claimed he was taught by God and distilled what he learned from his own personal discernment into his book *The Spiritual Exercises*.[3]

At the heart of the *Spiritual Exercises* was the discernment in one's heart of movements of consolation and desolation. The signs that we are living open to God's action Ignatius called "consolation":

> *By consolation I mean what occurs when some interior motion is caused within the soul through which it comes to be inflamed with love of its Creator and Lord. As a result it can love no created thing on the face of the earth in itself, but only in the Creator of them all. Similarly, this consolation is experienced when the soul sheds tears that move it to the love for its Lord— whether they are tears of grief for its own sins, or about the Passion of our Lord, or about other matters directly ordered to his service and praise. Finally under the word consolation I include every increase in faith, hope and charity, and every interior joy that calls and attracts one to heavenly things and to the salvation of one's soul, by bringing it tranquility and peace in its Creator and Lord.[4]*

The opposite of consolation Ignatius called "desolation": if our action brings with it deep feelings of sadness, depression, anxiety, and discontent, then that is a sign that what we are doing is wrong for us because it contradicts God's spirit within us.

Discerning Spirits in Our Hearts

Notice that all the texts on discernment speak of the location of the Spirit as "in our hearts." Both the Holy Spirit of God and the spirit of evil take up their abode in our hearts. The biblical distinction between heart and head is a distinction between feelings and thought. What is in our hearts can be discerned only by listening closely to our feelings. However, the reason why discernment may be a difficult practice for many gay people is because they have suppressed their feelings. Feelings are like a bowl of spaghetti, you can never get only one strand. If you allow yourself to feel one feeling, all the other feelings will be pulled in with it. You cannot experience the feeling of love without being ready to experience anger as well. The only way to suppress one feeling, for example, anger, is to suppress all feelings and try to live in your head.

Many gay people become distrustful and fearful of their gay feelings of attraction and affection. But as long as you are living in your head, trying to stay in control through dispassionate reason, you will miss what God is saying to you through your heart. The only way to practice discernment is to open up and trust your feelings. There is an ancient medieval saying: You can grasp God with your thought: never; you can grasp God with your heart: ever!

How often a seriously depressed gay client has come to me as therapist and told me a story of having fearfully hid in the closet for years. He had frequently gone out while drunk and had a one-night stand, hating himself for it when he woke up, hung over the next morning. His coming to therapy was occasioned by the fact that this time he went out while sober, met someone, and for the first time began to develop a healthy relationship. In the affectionate sexual exchange that followed soon afterward, he experienced the most profound feelings of joy, peace, and fulfillment he had ever known. But the next morning the old homophobic tapes, implanted by family, culture, and Church, began playing again in his head, telling him that he should despise and hate himself for what he did. (I term that internalized tape: *post-coitus tristis*.) He is tempted to cut off the relationship and go back to his old despairing closeted life-style, which usually involves compulsive acting out in one-night stands while drunk. Being drunk allows him to deny responsibility by blaming his alcoholic sickness, thus relieving the fear in his relationship to God. If he stayed in the sober relationship he would have to accept responsibility for it and change his image of God from one of fear to one of love.

How difficult it can be at times to get that client to discern spirits, to listen to his feelings and realize that God is saying something to him directly through those feelings of peace, joy, and fulfillment and, conversely, through the negative feelings of sadness, depression, and compulsive acting out. My hope as therapist and spiritual guide is that my client will be able to distinguish between his healthy gay needs and his longing for sexual intimacy, and the pathological need to try to deny and repress his gayness by repressing all need on his part for intimacy. "It is not good that a human remain alone. Every human has a need of a companion of his or her own kind!"[5] Gradually, my client should strive to learn to make his gay needs and his need for intimacy egosyntonic, that is, he should learn to accept and go with them and gradually lessen the power of the negative homophobic tapes in his head to control his life. In the words of a second-century Father of the Church, St. Irenaeus: "The glory of God are humans fully alive!" And that includes being fully alive sexually. The glory of God for a lesbian or gay man is to be fully alive as gay or lesbian.

Overcoming Fear through Discernment

In a recent article applying Ignatian spiritual discernment to the problems of youth in East Germany and broadening the application of those rules from the realm of the individual to the social, Thomas Gertler, S.J., makes some important points that, I believe, are equally valid in another context for gay Christians living in North America. Gertler asserts that the biggest problem was "our hidden and repressed interior freedom, resulting from the long sublimation of experiential fear." He points out that this fear is rooted less in the actual experience of repression than in the perceived possibility of terror, in feelings of powerlessness and abandonment, in the absence of rights and the lack of any opportunity to appeal for justice. "This overreaching fear expresses itself in a dampening of liveliness, a dimming of creativity. The rule was: 'Hold back, don't stick out, don't make waves.' "[6]

In my experience as a psychotherapist, I find a remarkable resemblance here to the kind of fear experienced by Christian gays who stay in the closet with, perhaps, the added dimension that gays also interiorize self-hatred to try to justify those fears. The foundation of "staying in the closet" is based in the projecting out of a paralyzing fear, a fear that leads to suppression of liveliness and creativity. As a result, Gertler writes, East Germans developed the strongest of inferiority complexes.

Why are we so afraid? The answer can be found in the relation of fear to power; those whom we fear have great power over us. Those who can make us afraid can also make us do what they want us to do. In order to be liberated from the control we must first bring into full consciousness this close connection between our fears and the power that others have over us. Gays and lesbians need to develop a conscious awareness of the destructive role of fear in their community. Our greatest enemy is not some outside opponent—it is the fear within us. The fear that we should seek to be liberated from is that kind of paranoid fear that impoverishes our conscience and cripples our response to those around us, numbing us to their needs because of anxiety about our own needs.

The first step toward liberation from that fear is to bring that fear and inner lack of freedom, which in all of us slips into the subconscious, clearly into consciousness. In his effort to control such fears, Gertler found the Ignatian "Rules for the Discernment of Spirits" a valuable help. The first of the Ignatian rules for discernment with which Gertler deals is the one in which Ignatius observed that subconscious fears feel irresistibly strong. But they are not. Evil pretends to be strong, but it is not naturally so. "I can know this from my own experience. After having failed at something, I think to myself: 'I will never be able to do this; I never improve; I am so undisciplined.' So I give up and give in, or I experience a downward spiral of failure after failure: 'There is no hope now; I have sunk far too deep ever to extract myself; I just don't care anymore.' "[7]

Such a spiral generates a self-perpetuating circle of impotence and apathy. We identify with our fears and allow them to become totally one with our ego. As a result they have complete control over us. If these fears are related to a struggle against evil, we begin to justify ourselves and cooperate with the powers that be: There is nothing to be done. There is no point in even trying. We all end up in the same cycle: giving in, playing ball, and forgetting all about our freedom, our possibilities, and our responsibilities.

People who live in fear never learned (never dared to learn) what they need most of all: initiative, decisiveness, the will to "show their colors." Like the East Germans, we gay people have been all too accustomed to the opposite: "Don't step out of line, don't speak first, wait and see what others are doing, test the waters." Our oppression is perpetuated by fear, mistrust, and an inability to believe in the goodness of human beings.

What advice does Ignatius give to those who have forgotten their own freedom and its functions? Use your freedom. Defend yourself from evil. Show determination. Never submit to fear; never make it egosyntonic. Never allow yourself to become totally a prisoner of fear. Every time you act in fear, the spirit of fear tightens its grip on you. Every time you take any action that contradicts your fears, you win a certain freedom from fear. And the next time, that action will be much easier.

That advice can be restated in these words: *I take the next possible step forward out of my fears*. This is a fundamental rule of the spiritual life and of psychological development. "In every instance, I am called to take the next peaceful step out of my enslavement to fear. The *next* step: I have to try to be concrete and pragmatic. *I* take it; whatever is within my ability, I can do. With God's help there is always some room for me to exercise freedom. The next possible *step*: I am not called on to leap or fly, but only to walk forward."[8] Ignatius was well aware that one of the tactics of the enemy is to tempt us to excess, to cause us to reach beyond our grasp and then, in the ensuing failure, to tighten his grip on us. Part of our discernment is to recognize what strengths and what graces are available to us now and to acknowledge our limits.

As soon as I begin to practice these first concrete steps, I will experience the inner growth of peace, confidence, hope, and joy. Indeed, with these steps I have already won a major victory, for I have recaptured my freedom and my ability to act. "If I do this within the context of the social order, then we all gain the same experience. We are not asleep, we are not simply cogs in the machine. We do have voices. We really can change things."[9]

Ignatius notes, "Our enemy may also be compared in his manner of acting to a false lover. He seeks to remain hidden and does not want to be discovered . . ."[10] In other words, evil always tries to camouflage itself. It wishes to remain secret. It lies. The primary instrument the spirit of evil uses to achieve its purpose is the spirit of fear. Whereas Jesus speaks of the indwelling Holy Spirit as desirous of leading us into all truth, Scripture speaks of Satan as "the Father of lies." The negative thoughts and feelings from the spirit of evil, when they remain trapped inside me, are powerful. I cannot get a hold on them. I cannot look at them, because I have not expressed them. And so they poison me. If I could utter them, if I could bring them up and speak them out, then they would become open to observation and I could do something about them.

The great power of the East German state, Gertler notes, lay in its ability to frighten everyone into living out a false self: "From kindergarten onward we learned that one was not allowed to say what one did or thought. . . . From the age of toddlers we have learned to keep our thoughts under lock and key, to hide ourselves away."[11] Gertler asks:

What were the consequences? They were and are very bad: I am able to bottle up my own opinion so completely that soon I cease to have one. This is a common phenomenon: Many people no longer know their own thoughts and feelings, for they can no longer bring them to expression. These two things are related. If I can no longer express my inner life, my inner self, it withers. I become less and less capable of expressing what I feel. . . . We don't have the vocabulary to express our finer, subtler feelings. In this, we have hurt ourselves badly. We have allowed a process of spiritual stultification to take place that has robbed us blind.[12]

"Evil," warned Dietrich Bonhoeffer, the German theologian who was hanged by the Nazis, "demands to have a man by himself. It withdraws him from community. The more isolated the person is, the more destructive will be the power of evil over him, the more disastrous his isolation. . . . Evil shuns the light. In the darkness of the unexpressed it poisons the whole being of a person."[13]

The power of the evil of homophobia is its ability to frighten the gay person to live in the closet and "live out a false self." Gay people who live in fear can so deny and repress their own thoughts and feelings until both wither up and they lose touch with their real identity.

What did Ignatius suggest that we do when faced with the hidden and lying Evil One? Expose it! Speak the truth! When I speak the truth I align myself with reality. For a gay person this speaking the truth can take the form of coming out of the closet to one's family or a friend. It takes a great deal of effort and pain to bring myself back into a correct relationship with reality, the type of relationship children have. This was the point of Jesus' words when he said: "If you do not become like little children, you shall never enter the Kingdom of God" (John 19: 13).

Gertler expresses a special concern for the Church:

> I have always experienced the Church as the place where more freedom, more openness and more preparedness for truth existed than in society at large. May it never come to pass that we lose this familiar Church, a Church in which we have such a foundational relationship of trust. May it never come to pass that there remain only isolated individuals in the Church with whom, either in the confessional or in spiritual conversation, I can speak my innermost truth and know that it will be received with love and reverence. May the Church itself as institution in all humility always place itself at the disposal of truth, which is greater even than the Church itself.[14]

This is one area where the gay person's experience differs sharply from that of Gertler. Throughout history, we have almost never found the Church to be a "place where more freedom, more openness and more preparedness for truth existed" concerning the issue of homosexuality. In fact, just the opposite, the Church was usually the place where there was the greatest threat and the greatest demand for self-hatred and repression. Traditionally homosexuality was referred to in the churches as "the sin that dare not speak its name." We were very lucky if we could find a confessor or spiritual guide with whom we could speak our innermost truth and be received compassionately, without judgment or rejection or being advised to deny and closet our reality.

Gertler makes a strong assertion concerning the need for and the value of humor.

> *One thing remained constant, the comic element of all this could not be acknowledged. This type of system is characterized by its total lack of humor. . . . When I can no longer recognize my own silliness, when I can no longer laugh at my foibles, then I am probably well on the way to neurosis. We fall into a trap every time we forget that we are not God and that we do not define the ultimate truth. Here we need a sense of humor. Indeed we humans can often overcome a difficult situation only through laughter or through tears, and not through the application of brute force.*

There is a strong parallel between Gertler's description of the role of humor in the totalitarian state and the use gays have made of humor to keep their sanity and make their "exile" more bearable. At its best, "gay camp" was always a means of affirming our dignity as human beings, while at the same time, laughing together at our foibles. "It is my ardent hope that we as a people can look back at the past—first with tears and then with laughter. When we have done this, then we will have reached the truth that sets us free."[15]

C H A P T E R 4

A CASE HISTORY *of*

DISCERNMENT *of* SPIRITS

The following is a case history of how one of my clients sought God's grace to be able to discern God's will for him as a gay man and a religious man under vows. (The client gave me permission to use his retreat notes in the hope that they could help others like him to be able to make a similar discernment. The names of places and people have been changed to protect the identity of my client.) The occasion of this discernment was a reading of Ezekiel, chapter 34, where Ezekiel calls the leaders of his church "false shepherds" because they use their power and authority primarily to secure their own position and authority and do not seek to take care of the needs of the people. God promises to take those people directly under his/her guidance and remove them from the jurisdiction of Church authorities.

> *The word of Yahweh was addressed to me as follows,*
> *"Son of man, prophesy against the shepherds of Israel;*
> *prophesy and say to them, Shepherds, the Lord Yah-*
> *weh says this: Disaster is in store for the shepherds of*
> *Israel who feed themselves! Are not shepherds meant*

to feed a flock? . . . You have failed to make weak sheep strong, or to care for the sick ones, or bandage the injured ones. You have failed to bring back strays or look for the lost. On the contrary, you have ruled them cruelly and harshly. For lack of a shepherd they have been scattered, to become the prey of all the wild animals; they have been scattered. . . .

"Very well, Shepherds, hear the word of Yahweh: As I live, I swear it—declares the Lord Yahweh . . . I am against the shepherds. I shall take my flock out of their charge and henceforth not allow them to feed my flock. And the shepherds will stop feeding themselves, because I shall rescue my sheep from their mouths to stop them from being food for them." (Ezek. 34:1–10)

My Client's Retreat Notes

I shall rescue my sheep from their mouths to stop them from being food for them.
                    Ezekiel 34:10

> *I had heard of conversion experiences and of God breaking into the lives of people, but at the age of fifty-eight and in my forty-first year of religious life, such a God was foreign to me. I was in desperate need of internal healing but knew in my heart that nothing so good could happen to me and even doubted that such things occurred to others.*
>
> *However, during an eight-day directed retreat in the silence of beautiful August summer days, my miracle happened. I received the precious grace to totally love and accept myself as the gay person whom God created me to be. After over fifty years of self-hate and shame the True Shepherd leapt from the pages of Ezekiel 34 to rescue me from the mouths of those who would want me to believe I am an abomination to my Creator. This True Shepherd bandaged my wound and made me strong. I am now part of the flock that He will watch over Himself.*

EARLY YEARS *I loved my Church while attending grammar school in the Western part of New York State. Our family had at-*

tained some stability in that area after having gone through a nomadic period previous to the enrollment of the five of us at the parish school run by the Sisters of St. Joseph. I was a familiar face around the Church—boy soprano in the choir and the ever-faithful always-available altar boy. My mother made me a full set of vestments, and neighbors heard me preach the Sunday sermon from my upstairs room.

This charmed relationship with the Church was to change as I entered puberty. I can vaguely remember an incident after responding to a call in the seventh grade to try out for the school basketball team. After the workout, too embarrassed to take a shower myself, I looked into the shower area as I was leaving the locker room. I don't remember exactly what was said by the coach who confronted me at that time, but it made a deep and lasting impression. I never came back to another practice session and never participated in any school sports for the rest of my academic career, although it was a high interest area for me. I knew I felt I did something very wrong and I was a bad person.

HIGH SCHOOL   At the end of my eighth grade we moved to downstate New York, and I was registered at a high school taught by religious brothers. My connection with the Church was never the same. It now became for me a place where I confessed my sexual thoughts and masturbatory actions to receive forgiveness until the next Saturday. It was a cycle of shame and guilt with momentary peace. In addition, I realized I was attracted to some of the other male students at school. This I never mentioned to anyone. I knew this was wrong and made me a bad person. I had no name to put on it and felt it was something very unique to myself.

RELIGIOUS LIFE   The sheltered and over-protected life I experienced in my family and twelve years of Catholic schooling helped me make a smooth transition to religious life. Preoccupation with sexual thoughts and masturbation ceased during my Novitiate year only to return with a vengeance during the rest of my formative training. My same-sex attraction not only continued but intensified. It was my secret with one exception. Over a period of three years, I ran from a strong mutual attraction with a classmate who on and off wished to pursue it with me. My paralyzing fear prevented me from acting on this.

Leaving the confinement of formative training and embarking on my teaching mission helped to relieve much of the stress I was experiencing. For the next twenty-four years, I threw myself totally into my identity as brother and teacher, finding satisfaction in my work. But the deepest core of my being was in constant turmoil. I was attracted to many of my students which only heightened my anxiety and fear. The cycle of shame, guilt, and confession continued over the years. I kept my secret. No one else could possibly be experiencing any of this. I am uniquely a bad person.

Alcohol helped ease some of the pain. I needed my drink each evening before supper to get me through the night. On the outside all was well. If you work hard in the brothers you are easily accepted. I was a workaholic. I had no identity of my own. I had no idea who I was, nor did I know that this would be worth something to find out.

A BREAKTHROUGH   My True Shepherd touched my life again in a mysterious way. It became clear to me that I was dying in the classroom. It was no longer life-giving but was draining me emotionally and physically. Despite hours of meticulous preparation, I felt inadequate and sensed a growing alienation from the students. I wrote my Provincial that I needed to leave teaching. I did not know what I would do; neither did he.

I now was embarking on a journey into the depths of my soul. A place where I never wanted to go and I could not go alone. Providentially six months previously I had made reservations for a thirty-day contemplative experience at a remote location. This solitude was my initiation into being alone with myself.

My second step was a nine-month Clinical Pastoral Education residency program at a hospital. A CPE program helps you get in touch with those areas of your life which are blocks to your ministry to others. It was my stepping stone to my next twelve years of ministry—eight years as a hospital chaplain and four years in AIDS ministry.

THE JOURNEY   Why was I called on this journey? My True Shepherd knew my brokenness. Along with my ministry I plunged into continuing psychotherapy. For twelve years, I was involved in both small group and individual therapy. I dealt with the endless areas of concern, issue by issue. Each person has their own path, their own process, and their own time.

I experienced a freedom during that period of time which I had *never experienced before. I was not living in one of our religious communities. Living alone forced me to live with myself and learn who I was.*

Along with my therapy I sought spiritual direction. For ten years, I was gifted with two directors who helped me let go of the image of God I was taught and to slowly replace it with the image of God that Jesus shared with us. It was my need to disconnect from the institutional Church and trust that my True Shepherd would find me and bring me back to the flock where He would be on watch.

It is incredible that during most of this journey my same-sex attraction did not surface as a therapy issue. By letting go of the institutional Church I was able to let go of much of my shame and guilt. Being away from community and school removed me from a familiar setting where these issues more readily surfaced as a problem to be addressed. It was still my secret and I did not have a name for it.

NAMING IT! *Then something happened that brought this issue to the surface for me. I became conscious of people dying with AIDS while doing my work in the hospitals. I volunteered to become a buddy for a state-wide AIDS organization and was assigned a gay man to care for. My True Shepherd was working overtime. It was in this encounter that I became fully aware of who I was. I now had a name for these feelings, and I was experiencing an incredible love for this gay man. He became my teacher.*

I slowly and tentatively began to come out to friends, some family members, some brothers, and the people in my small therapy group. I also was aware that I was paralyzed with fear and could not accept myself as I was. The homophobic voices of Church and society did not make it easier. "For lack of a shepherd they have been scattered. . . . My flock is astray on every mountain. . . . I shall take my flock out of their charge. . . . I myself shall take care of my flock and look after it" (Ezek. 34:5–11).

EPILOGUE *As I mentioned at the beginning, my True Shepherd invited me through my spiritual director to spend eight days under His care in rich pastures over a year ago. At this time an internal healing of my self-hatred began to take place. Since then I have learned we cannot live on the mountaintop but must do daily battle against negative voices.*

CALLED TO BE HEALED *My True Shepherd once again touched my life and invited me through my director to spend eight quiet days under His care in rich pastures. As I mentioned earlier it was there I was healed of my deepest wounds. How can one put that into words? One can only try.*

My retreat guidelines were: Get in touch with who you are and bring that person into the presence of God; from all eternity God has chosen this time to be with you; all you need to do is show up; let go of any expectations. Early in the retreat it became clear to me that I was being asked to know who I was in my deepest being and to accept that God had created me as a gay man.

One morning I was so in touch in oneness with my body. I experienced it as something beautiful and good—with sexual and alive feelings. All was good and God was present. Later that day it felt so right that my body was good and was an instrument for giving and receiving love.

It became clear to me that I was in need of a lover in my life.

> *It is time to turn one's back to the violent Church and*
> *not listen to this voice—it is not the voice of God.*
> *The Shepherd's voice*
> *gives life*
> *gives peace*
> *gives hope*
> *and is not destructive of nature.*
> *I have come that you may have life*
> *and may live it to the full.*
> *Having a lover is life for me.*
> *I know this is my need.*
> *I need this to live life to the full.*

I listen for the guilt and the fear to return, but they are not present. Only feelings of peace and joy remain. My deepest wound is revealed to me: I DID NOT BELIEVE ANYONE, INCLUDING GOD, COULD LOVE ME FOR MYSELF.

> *I have always felt that I was a bad person because*
> *of my sexual desires, sexual thoughts, and*
> *masturbation.*
> *I have put up a wall around me, to keep people*

*away, including my God. I am in desperate need
of healing.*

*It became clear to me that my healing would come
when I slept with another human being,
preferably a man for me.*

*I desperately need to be touched, skin against skin,
and feel the warmth of another human being in
my life.*

*This is the desperate need of a human being deprived
of all human touch and human warmth for fifty-
nine years.*

*It is the desperate cry of one who can no longer keep
human beings out of his life.*

*This is not about sexuality or celibacy but breathing
life into a dying body.*

*Yet, I welcome sexuality for it will bring me life—I
need to feel cared for, feel loved.*

This is where my healing lies.

Why cannot a brother give this to another brother?

What is celibacy?

*Should this prevent us from giving life to one
another?*

Are we to watch each other die of loneliness?

*Are we to watch each other become bitter old men
who have kept their vow?*

I know what I need for my healing.

*Please, God, give me the courage to ask for it from
my brothers or another human being.*

*We all need to receive God's love, no matter what it
looks like.*

At the end of the retreat, it came to me that isn't that what my
gift of gayness is? Is it not God's love for me? And should I not receive it and
live it to the full no matter what it looks like to others? "I myself shall pas-
ture my sheep, I myself shall give them rest. . . . I shall look for the lost one,
bring back the stray, bandage the injured and make the sick strong. . . . I
shall be a true shepherd to them" (Ezek. 34:15–16).

Reflections on the Case History

My client has continued on his healing path since that retreat. He has come out to his family and to his religious order, and he is actively seeking out gay friends and companions. In many ways this very moving case history is unique, as is the person whose history it is. At the same time, however, it reveals the same basic pattern of recovery that many of my clients, especially those from a strong religious background, have had to pass through in order to succeed in coming out of the closet, positively accepting their gayness, and laying the foundation for a healthy gay relationship. One cannot found a healthy relationship on an aspect of the self one hates and is ashamed of.

The first step in this typical process is the interiorization of the homophobia of family, church, and culture. In the past this almost always led to the feeling of being different, of being the only one in the world with these feelings. This in turn leads to a total suppression of one's gay identity, using pathological religious concepts of fear and shame to achieve that repression. Having suppressed all feelings, the individual tries to live "out of the head," developing intellectual skills that are conflict free, burying themselves in their studies and work. They base their identity on their ability to meet the needs of others while repressing and denying their own needs. Many from a Catholic background will, frequently unconsciously, use a vocation to celibate religious life to avoid having to deal at all with sexuality and intimacy. Sooner or later this process of self-denial and repression will bottom out with serious depression, rage, and on frequent occasions serious alcohol or drug abuse, compulsive acting out of needs for intimacy, affection, and sexual fulfillment leading to greater shame, guilt, and fear, sometimes resulting in psychological breakdown and even efforts at suicide.

The client in this case history bottomed out with serious depression, which led him to take the courageous action of seeking out individual and group therapy, fortunately with a gay positive therapist. He also had the good fortune to be aware that secular therapy alone would not be adequate to meet his needs. He also had to find a way to mature spiritually.

Through competent spiritual directors he began the process of learning how to discern spirits and hear the voice of God speaking to him in his heart directly through his experiences and feelings. He began the process of sorting out his pathological religious feelings from his healthy mature experience of God's love for him and began building a healthy religious relationship with the God of love. To achieve that growth he had to risk taking distance from the institutional Church's authority.

My client had to go through several years of healing psychotherapy and spiritual direction before he was ready to safely address the issue of his gay identity. That breakthrough occurred for him by falling in love with a man with AIDS for whom he was a buddy. The deep peace and joy he experienced in that love was his first step toward a positive acceptance of his gayness.

But the struggle to heal the wound of his self-hatred was not over. At every step of the process my client sought God's help through prayer, retreats, and spiritual direction. He made a wise application of the saying of Ignatius: We must pray as if everything depended on us. We must act as if everything depended on God!

CHAPTER 5

My PERSONAL EXPERIENCE

of DISCERNMENT

In 1977, I was ordered to silence by the Vatican on the issue of homosexuality. This order came as the result of the publication of my book *The Church and the Homosexual*, which argued that loving gay or lesbian relationships between consenting adults should be acceptable in the Church. Since I was given that order formally under the vow of obedience to which I had freely committed myself on entering the Society of Jesus, all my spiritual training led me to accept that order and obey. And for almost a decade, I did my best to abide by that order to silence. I did not speak publicly or write anything concerning homosexuality. I was allowed, however, to continue my ministry to lesbians and gays, preaching, giving retreats and workshops, as long as that did not involve challenging Catholic Church teaching in the public media (see appendix 2 for further detail on the Vatican's response to my book *The Church and the Homosexual*).

That same decade, 1978–1988, saw the spread of AIDS and a growing political attack on the rights of gay people, an attack which increasingly had the explicit support of the hierarchy of the Catholic Church. Every day, I resubmitted my silence to God, asking that God's spirit guide me. At times, I saw my silence as completely in accord with the Holy Spirit, and my desire to speak out as an ego trip, my desire to be in the limelight. At other times, I felt that my obedience was primarily based in fear of the consequences and that I was betraying those whom God had called me to serve because of my selfish needs for security and acceptance in the Church. I saw no way out of that dilemma until the Holy Spirit took matters into her own hands and I received a further order from Rome.

In November 1985, two months after my address on the subject of freedom of conscience at the National Dignity Convention in New York City, I was called in by my Jesuit Provincial, the superior of all the Jesuits in the New York Province. Because of complaints from the local hierarchy concerning my questioning of the Catholic Church's teaching concerning homosexuality, Cardinal Ratzinger of the Congregation for the Defense of the Faith (previously called the Holy Inquisition, this Congregation is charged with defending Church teaching in matters of faith and morals) had called in the General of the Society of Jesus, the Society's highest authority, and given him an order he was to pass on to me. I was to "withdraw from any and all ministry to homosexual persons." Father General Peter Hans Kolvenbach expressed a willingness to allow me to continue my private ministry of psychotherapy, for which he expressed "a sincere respect and value." However, he absolutely forbade me to take part in any public way in public ministry to gay people. I was not to be associated in any way with gay causes, including passive attendance at a meeting or liturgy. He also made it clear that if my private ministry of psychotherapy came to public attention, he could not guarantee that the Congregation would agree to my continuing even that.

I spent several months in prayer and consultation with spiritual advisors to try to discern what God wanted me to do. There were two key moments that helped me reach a decision during those difficult months of discernment. The first was the advice of a former Jesuit Provincial and spiritual guide. After I described to him all the pros and cons I had been debating, he suggested that I was going about the discernment process all wrong. I was too much in my head. He told me that if he went outside his apartment in the South Bronx and saw someone lying at the curb, and asked what was wrong, and was told he or she had no food and no bed to sleep in, then he knew what God was asking of him—to find food and shelter for this poor human being. Because of my gayness and my pastoral experience, God had put me in touch, on both a personal and pastoral level, with the special pain and suffering of gay people. Then it was perfectly clear that God was calling me to relieve those sufferings in any way I could, regardless of the consequences.

My advisor also recalled for me the meditation all Jesuits make on what Ignatius called "the three degrees of humility." Ignatius saw these as three steps into a closer identity and intimacy with Jesus. "Humility lies in the acceptance of Jesus Christ as the fullness of what it means to be human."[1] Ignatius is echoing the words of Paul that we are all called to "form the perfect Man, fully mature with the fullness of Christ himself" (Eph. 4:13).

"To be humble is to live as close to the truth as possible: that I am created in the likeness of Christ, that I am meant to live according to the pattern of his paschal mystery, and that my whole fulfillment is found in being near to Christ as he draws me to himself."[2]

In the first degree of humility, St. Ignatius suggests that I ask God's grace never to consider any action that would separate me from God and Jesus even if my life depended on it. "I would want to do nothing that would cut me off from God—not even if I were made head of all creation or even just to save my own life here on earth. I know that grave sin in this sense is to miss the whole meaning of being a person—one who is created and redeemed and is destined to live forever in love with God, my Creator and Lord."[3]

The second degree is to seek the grace to be indifferent to a long life or a short one, to honors or to disgrace, to pleasure or to suffering in order to be free to do whatever Jesus wants of me. "My life is firmly grounded in the fact that the reality of being a person is seen fully in Jesus Christ. Just as 'I have come to do your will, O God' is the motivating force of his life, so the only real principle of choice in my life is to seek out and do the will of the Father. With this habitual attitude, I find I can maintain a certain balance in my inclinations to have riches rather than poverty, honor rather than dishonor, or to desire a long life rather than a short one. I would not want to turn away from God even in small ways, because my whole desire is to respond ever more faithfully to his call."[4]

The third degree is most perfect humility, namely, "in order to imitate and be more actually like Christ our Lord, I want and choose poverty with Christ poor rather than riches, opprobrium with Christ replete with it rather than honors; and to desire to be rated as worthless and a fool for Christ, Who first was held as such, rather than wise and prudent in this world."[5]

In a note Ignatius acknowledges that this third degree is a special grace, a gift that comes primarily from God's initiative. He recommends, at this point, that one return in prayer to the Colloquy which reads: "First, I approach our Lady, asking her to obtain for me from her Son the grace-gift to follow him in the highest spiritual poverty, and should God be pleased thereby and want to choose and accept me, even in actual poverty. Even greater is the gift I seek in being able to bear the insults and the contempt of my world, so imitating Christ, my Lord ever more closely . . ."[6]

David Fleming, S.J., has reworded the third degree:

> . . . I so much want the truth of Christ's life to be the truth of my own that I find myself, moved by grace, with a love and a desire for poverty in order to be with the poor Christ; a love and a desire for insults in order to be closer to Christ in his own rejection by people; a love and a desire to be considered worthless and a fool for Christ, rather than to be esteemed as wise and prudent according to the standards of the world. By grace, I find myself so moved to follow Jesus Christ in the most intimate union possible, that his experiences are reflected in my own. In that, I find my delight.[7]

As a young man in novitiate at Saint-Andrew-on-Hudson, I vividly remember my very strong reaction to this third degree and feeling that I was not ready to go that far. I realize now that the strength of my reaction was based in the fact that I was still relating to a god of fear. When I read the words in Revelation to John: "Amen; come, Lord Jesus!" (Rev. 22:20), I spontaneously prayed, "Wait, Lord Jesus! Wait!" I was not ready for the kind of intimacy Ignatius sought because I was not yet open to such a deep and radical loving intimacy with my God.

Still, I followed the advice of Ignatius and made the triple colloquy, praying to Mary, her son Jesus, and the Father that someday, when I was ready, to grant me the grace to grow into and experience that kind of passionate desire for the deepest possible union and intimacy with the Lord.

Little did I know that following out my decision in conscience to continue my ministry to lesbians and gays would be the occasion for me to receive an answer to that young novice's prayers and have a very real experience of the third degree.

The second moment that helped me reach my decision occurred while I spent a week at the Trappist monastery Gethsemani in Kentucky. One day during holy week while I was in prayer, agonizing over the decision which was due that weekend, a knock came at the door of my room, and a monk with a great red beard whom I did not know and had never seen before handed me a slip of paper. On that paper was written the Buddhist vow of compassion, *The Bodhisattva's Vow of Universal Redemption*. He explained to me that a Bodhisattva is one who, after attaining enlightenment, defers her or his entrance into nirvana (that is, cessation of the cycle of birth and death) and chooses instead to continue being born in a human body in order to share the burden of others' sufferings and sorrows, and to aid them by her or his compassionate presence. Sharing the suffering of the human state, the Bodhisattva freely chooses "exile" until all human beings can enter into salvation. The vow reads:

> *I take upon myself the burden of my suffering brothers {and sisters}, I am resolved to do so. I will endure it. I will not turn or run away. I will not turn back. I cannot.*

> *And why? My endeavors do not merely aim at my own deliverance. I must help all my brothers {and sisters} cross the stream of this life which is so difficult to cross. With the help of the boat of compassion I must help them across the stream. I would fain become a soother of all the sorrows of my brothers {and sisters}. May I be a balm to those who are sick, their healer and*

servant until sickness come never again. May I become
an unfailing store for my poor brothers {and sisters}
and serve them in their need. May I be in the famine
at the ages' end, their drink and their meat.

My own being, all my life, all my spirituality in the
past, present and future I surrender that my brothers
{and sisters} may win through to their end, for they
dwell in my spirit.[8]

The spirit of this vow is exactly the spirit being lived out by thousands of gay and lesbian people as well as many others who have dedicated themselves as volunteers to do whatever they can to relieve the suffering of persons with AIDS. I was struck by the statement the actor Anthony Perkins made just a few days before his death from AIDS: "There are many that believe that this disease is God's vengeance, but I believe it was sent to teach people how to love and understand and have compassion for each other. I have learned more about love, selflessness and human understanding from the people I have met in this great adventure in the world of AIDS than I ever did in the cutthroat, competitive world in which I spent my life."[9]

This Buddhist vow brought back to mind the spiritual meaning of Christ's life, the quality of compassion, expressed in my favorite text in Scripture:

Make your own the mind of Christ Jesus:
Who, being in the form of God,
did not count equality with God
something to be grasped.

But he emptied himself,
taking the form of a slave,
becoming as human beings are;
and being in every way
    like a human being,
he was humbler yet,

even to accepting death,
death on a cross.

And for this God raised him high,
and gave him the name
which is above all other names;

so that . . .
. . . every tongue should acknowledge
Jesus Christ as Lord,
to the glory of God the Father. (Phil. 2:5–11)

Whenever I prayed over the possibility of obeying the order I received from Rome to give up all ministry to lesbians and gays, my spirit was troubled and I had a strong feeling that I did not have the right in conscience to abandon the gay community which had turned to me for help and guidance. In the course of my ten years of silence in obedience to Rome, my understanding of how to discern the will of God changed, I hope, for the better. It had grown and matured under the constant pressure of trying to do God's will within the confines of re-strictive directives from Rome. Roman authorities were inclined to see my efforts to interpret the restrictions on my freedom in the narrowest of possible ways as revealing too "legalistic" an attitude and as playing games with obedience. I saw my efforts as an honest attempt to try to put together my obedience to the orders I received from Rome with my obedience to the will of God calling me to a ministry of compassion to gay people. I kept in mind a legal principle I learned from my teacher of Canon Law: *Odiosa sint restringenda* (Restrictive laws are to be narrowly interpreted).

As Edward Schillebeeckx observes in his book *Ministry: Leadership in the Community of Jesus Christ*: "Christian obedience is also listening so as to be involved in the *kairos* of the moment of grace of a particular time, listening in obedience to the suffering of human beings and the seeds of a Christian community, and then performing specific actions in conformity with that 'voice of God.' This is also and above all a fundamental form of Christian obedience, derived from the authority of human beings who are suffering and in need." Schillebeeckx goes on to observe that where this form of obedience comes into conflict with authority, Thomas Aquinas allows that a human's conscience which has been tested in such a conflict (and not just because it is sure of itself) is free to make a decision contrary to authority and, moreover, adds that a conscientious person must do this "even if he knows that as a result he can be excommunicated by the Church."[10]

God had granted me that grace, an intimate awareness of the suffering and of the seeds of community among my gay brothers and lesbian sisters. First of all, I knew my own sufferings as a gay man and as a gay priest. My struggles to reconcile my faith and trust in God with my self-acceptance and my ministry to gay people, including my work as a psychotherapist with hundreds of gay clients, had put me in intimate contact with the special psychological pain most gay people suffer in our culture and especially in the Catholic Church. I became intensely aware that, unless we are dealing with a sadistic God, what is destructive psychologically for so many people has to be bad theology!

Not only was there great suffering for individual men and women, but also for the gay community at large. The massive crucifixion of AIDS has rivaled in its virulence any plague of the Middle Ages. According to experts AIDS threatens the life of one out of two gay men, and this plague leads to a lingering death, frequently with terrible pain and disfigurement. This suffering is compounded by mass hysteria and fear that lead to persecution and hideous injustice by the community at large. I understood that the special gifts—gifts of understanding, self-acceptance as a gay man, and confidence in God's love and mercy—that God has given to me were there so that I could share them with others like myself. I could become an instrument of God's compassion.

Although I was leaning toward deciding to disobey the Vatican order, I was aware that my decision might be wrong, that subtle forms of egoism and self-deceit might be influencing it. I was also aware, however, that fear and the urge to be secure within the Church and the Jesuit Society should not deter me from bearing witness from within the Church to what I thought and felt was the truth. I had to trust that if I were wrong, God would make my error known to me and the Holy Spirit would protect those whom my error might endanger. If my decision were right, good consequences would flow from it in the lives of those to whom I ministered.

I have frequently preached to my gay family that we must be prepared to "embrace ourselves as exiles." We must be prepared to accept our exiled state both within society and in the Church. We must grieve and gradually let go of the desire to "belong" to all the institutions of this world. We must deepen our spiritual roots and our realization that, in direct proportion to our exiled status in this world, we belong on a deeper and more cosmic level to a community bound together by God's love and mercy. I knew that the decision to continue my public ministry would require me to learn to practice what I had been preaching on an even more profound level.

Finally it was clear to me what my decision must be. I wrote to my religious superior in 1985: "God has called me to a ministry of compassion to gay people and I cannot in conscience renounce that ministry."

That refusal to obey the Vatican's latest order brought with it a rather surprising grace of real peace and joy. I had struggled for nine years to discern whether my silence was following the will of God according to my vows as a Jesuit, or if it were instead cowardice and fear of the consequences of disobedience. I also was not certain that my decision to speak out and disobey my orders was not influenced by pure egoism and a desire to be in the limelight. But I hoped and prayed that God was calling me to speak out and accept the consequences of being separated from my religious family and from my legal right to exercise my priesthood. I believe this was my personal call to the "third degree of humility."

I became convinced that gay people needed a spokesperson and defender in the Catholic Church who from personal experience could fearlessly speak the truth about gayness.

I brought my decision once more before God for a final discernment during a retreat at Mount Saviour monastery near Elmira, New York. During prayer, I had the distinct impression that God was annoyed with me for badgering Him/Her for further evidence. The answer I seemed to get from God was: "Leave me alone; I don't care what you do. You choose and I will go with you down whichever path you choose!"

I remember praying excitedly: If that is so, God, I have no doubt what I would like to choose! Again, the answer I got was: "Go ahead, choose and I will go with you!" God is certainly full of surprises. I broke my silence with a press release in November 1986, and the final decree of dismissal from the Jesuits was issued in April 1987.

My decision has not been without costs. I was expelled from my religious order, which had been my home and family for forty years. I ended up in my old age without any pension or insurance. I was deprived of my right to exercise my priesthood. My reputation and character were publicly attacked by the Vatican (see appendix 2). At the same time, God's grace made that experience one of peace and joy, rather than pain and desolation. I have experienced my life since that time as productive and joyfully free and full of a deep experience of God's loving presence.

One year after my dismissal I returned for my annual retreat to Mount Saviour monastery. I anticipated a quiet retreat, untroubled by any need to discern, during which I would express my gratitude to God. To my surprise, I no sooner placed myself in the presence of God and began to pray when an unexpected question popped into my mind: *Where will I be buried?* This is typically an Irish question. For some reason, death and the last things have always been of primary concern to the Irish. I still remember that the greatest compliment the Irish priest of my childhood could pay was to wish you a large funeral. Every morning, I open my newspaper first to the obituary page, the Irish *scratch sheet* I like to call it. If I were still a member of the Jesuit order, I would be buried in the Jesuit graveyard of the New York Province at the Shrine of the North American Jesuit Martyrs in Auriesville. While still a member, I used to go there, estimate where I would be buried, lie down on the ground, and get the feel of it. I thought that there could be no better place and no better companions with whom to greet the resurrection.

It dawned on me as I prayed that I was not only expelled from the order, but from the order's graveyard as well. Tears welled in my eyes as that realization dawned on me, and I began to mourn my separation from the Jesuits in a new and deeper way. I remember praying: *Well, God, you really have no mercy on a gay man! Not only are we exiles in this world, we are exiles even in death!* I believe I went through the deepest and most painful experience of mourning at that time. That evening,

I called my family in Buffalo to see if there was any room for me in the family plot. There wasn't. The next morning I visited the public grave-yard at the monastery. There was a delightful statue of Jesus as an ad-olescent bringing home the lost sheep. Jesus and the sheep both had big smiles on their faces. I decided then and there to ask permission from the Abbot to be buried there, but the Abbot informed me with sorrow that the cemetery was over-subscribed.

I thought about cremation, so I called my lover and com-panion of the last twenty-nine years, Charlie, and asked him, "If I were cremated and left you my ashes, what would you do with them?" Charlie told me he would put my ashes in the trunk of his car and when, sur-prised, I asked why, he said that if he ever got stuck on the ice he would ask me for one last favor. Charlie's sense of humor was a good tonic for me. I returned once again to prayer and suddenly I envisioned my gravestone:

> *Here Lies a Gay Priest*
> *Who Took a Chance on God!*
> *John J. McNeill 1925–?*

The image of that gravestone filled me with peace and joy. I could have the last word etched in stone, so to speak. I could preach my message from the grave. Then the question arose: Where could I put that stone? After another period of prayer, I realized that the perfect place would be the memorial garden at Kirkridge Retreat Center, where the ashes of those who died from AIDS can be scattered. I have given retreats for gays and lesbians at Kirkridge for eighteen years now, fre-quently twice a year. That made it the perfect spot for my "last word" to be spoken. The trustees at Kirkridge have agreed to my request.

God has left me no doubt that my decision was the right one. Shortly after my dismissal, now more than eight years ago, Walter Wink, the Biblical theologian, wrote me these prophetic words: "John, when the Vatican imprudently slammed the door on you, the gust of wind it set off blew open hundreds of doors. In the craftiness of God, I swear, your impact will be increased exponentially." Two honors I have received in 1993 give an indication of how true Wink's prediction was. The first was a Special Award given me by the Metropolitan Community

Church at its sixteenth international congress in Phoenix, Arizona, in July 1993 honoring me for "bringing the message of the gospel to gay and lesbian people everywhere."

The second was the Distinguished Contribution Award presented to me in November 1993 by the Eastern Region of The American Association of Pastoral Counselors, an interdenominational group of clergy who are also professional psychotherapists. The award reads:

> *Our region has been enriched by your healing presence and skillful practice of pastoral psychotherapy.*
>
> *By your wisdom imparted as supervisor, author, and teacher of pastoral psychotherapy and spiritual direction,*
>
> *By your prophetic message to us from gays and lesbians who have discovered their spiritual gifts and who call us to live justly and to worship the God of Love.*

My spirit is filled with gratitude to God who led me through the Spirit into self-acceptance as a gay man and through a series of decisions that have made me available to joyfully carry on God's ministry to my lesbian sisters and gay brothers. Thanks be to God!

P A R T   2

COMING OUT: THE
THREE STAGES
OF HOMOSEXUAL
HOLINESS

INTRODUCTION

The GAY SELF *and*
the CATHOLIC HIERARCHY

       In Part 2, I will deal with the three-stage process of coming out that I understand is necessary in order to create the authentic gay self. The Catholic Church agrees with the religious right on what constitutes a "moral" gay life: staying in the closet and repressing all desires for intimacy and sexual fulfillment. After twenty-five years of practicing psychotherapy with gay and lesbian clients, I am convinced that anyone who follows the Church program will end by destroying themselves in terms of both mental health and spiritual maturity. ▼ Just a few weeks prior to the notorious G.O.P. convention of August 1992 which was dominated by antigay speeches of the religious right, the Vatican issued a document addressed to all the bishops of the world entitled "Some Considerations Concerning the Catholic Response to Legislative Proposals on the Non-Discrimination of Homosexual Persons."[1] Since the political agenda outlined in this document is identical to that of the far right in the United States, I cannot believe that the timing was coincidental. It was embarrassing and painful for me and thousands of other gay Catholics to read a homophobic political statement cloaked in moralistic language issued by the highest authorities of our Church. The intention of that document was to advise the American bishops on how to oppose legislation supporting gay rights, on the grounds that any support would imply acceptance of the "immoral" gay life-style. ▼ For those of us who are Catholic and gay, who love the Church and see it as our spiritual family, the Vatican document is profoundly cruel in that it lacks any pastoral understanding or compassion for the pain and suffering of gay people. This lack is particularly egregious in this time of the AIDS epidemic, when thousands of gay Catholics have a profound need for the loving, nonjudgmental pastoral support of their Church. On the contrary, in a very paranoid spirit, the Vatican document seems to suggest that any effort on the part of gay people to achieve their legitimate rights, or to create a social space where they can live healthy, happy, and holy lives, is an organized conspiracy to destroy family values. The document makes mean-spirited and hysterical accusations such as these: that gays are involved in an effort "to *manipulate* the Church by gaining the often well-intentioned support of her pastors with a view to changing civil statutes and laws," and that "this [effort] is done in order to conform to these *pressure groups'* concept that homosexuality is at least a completely harmless, if not an entirely good, thing."[2] ▼ The 1992 document claims to draw logical political conclusions that flow from a previous letter issued in October 1986 by Cardinal Ratzinger, head of the Congregation for the Doctrine of the Faith, entitled "Letter to the Bishops of the Catholic Church on the Pastoral Care of Homosexual Persons."[3] This 1986 letter provoked intense criticisms by both theologians and professional psychotherapists. Theological critics pointed out its unscholarly use of "proof texts" in Scripture. (Proof texts are texts lifted out of their context and whose meaning is distorted, in this case, to carry an antihomosexual message.) They also criticized its highly debatable use of a biologically based understanding of human nature. Psychotherapists criticized its ignorance of the psychological nature of homosexuality and the developmental needs of homosexual persons. The Catholic gay community found it wanting because of its failure to recognize the need for the Church to enter into dialogue with gay and lesbian Catholics to be able to hear what the Holy Spirit is saying to the Church through their experience. ▼ Gay and lesbian Catholics have been offering the Church this dialogue for the past twenty years through organizations such as Dignity, but the hierarchy has responded by refusing to allow Dignity chapters to use Church property for their meetings. Sometimes we gay Catholics feel like the child of whom the Bible speaks who asks Mother Church for bread but is handed a scorpion instead. ▼ The 1992 Vatican document does not acknowledge or respond to any of the critiques of the Ratzinger letter, much less disavow its most extreme statements. For example, Ratzinger's letter claimed that, if homosexuals continue to demand "unthinkable" civil rights, then they have themselves to blame for the violence of gay-bashers. This statement has been interpreted in some quarters as encouraging violence against gay people. Similarly, Cardinal Ratzinger's letter hinted that it is those who work for gay rights and those professionals who try to help gays to a life of healthy self-acceptance who are responsible for the AIDS epidemic. He stated, "Even when the practice of homosexuality may seriously threaten the lives and well-

being of a large number of people, its advocates remained un-
deterred and refuse to consider the magnitude of the risks involved."[4] ▼ From my experience in pastoral ministry with
thousands of Catholic gays, I know that Ratzinger's claim is
unjustified. In fact, the persons most likely to end up compulsively acting out their sexual needs in an unsafe way and
therefore exposing themselves to the HIV virus are precisely
those Catholic gay men who have internalized the self-hatred
that Catholic Church teaching imposes on them. They frequently are the ones who find it impossible to suppress and
deny their sexual needs; at the same time, because of that internalized self-hatred, they cannot enter into a healthy, open,
and committed intimacy with anyone. ▼ In a recent letter to
the *New York Times* (September 2, 1992), Richard Isay, the
chairman of the American Psychiatric Association Committee
on gay, lesbian, and bisexual affairs, points out that the
suppression of sexuality, whether by religion, the state, or
therapists who make unsubstantiated claims to be able to
change homosexuals to heterosexuals, does significant dam-
age to the self-esteem of gay men and lesbians.[5] It subverts
their capacity to express their sexuality in mutually loving relationships. Hatred and rejection contribute to the high suicide
rate of gay and lesbian youth, estimated by the Department of
Health and Human Services task force in their 1989 report to
be 30 percent of all youth suicides in the United States.[6]
▼ The European regional office of the World Health Organization stated in 1991: "Unresolved personal attitudes and social conflicts . . . are themselves important contributions to
individual health problems. People who hide their sexual orientation for fear of discrimination or alienation have less fulfilling lives, encounter stress and are placed in situations that
are not conducive to safe sex practices."[7] Isay makes the point

that a consensus is growing among mental health professionals that homophobia, the irrational fear and hatred of homosexuals, is a psychological abnormality that interferes with the judgment and reliability of those affected. ▼ The 1992 Vatican directive claims that discrimination against homosexuals is not unjust in areas such as employment, housing, adoption and foster care of children, and service in the military. For example, it makes an empirically unverified statement that "homosexual activity prevents one's own fulfillment and happiness by acting contrary to the creative wisdom of God."[8] All empirical evidence of which I am aware points in exactly the opposite direction. The vast majority of those who attempt to live lives without any sexual intimacy, who internalize selfhatred of their gayness and stay in the closet, end up profoundly unhappy, are frequently suicidal, and usually run into very serious psychological problems that frequently lead to alcoholism, drug abuse, and mental breakdown. ▼ On the other hand, those gays who learn to accept and love their gayness, undertake therapy to heal their own internalized homophobia, and come out of the closet at least to those whom they love have the best chance of living out healthy and happy lives. What is bad psychology has to be bad theology and vice versa. Lesbian and gay Catholics must, in conscience, refuse a life-style which requires staying in the closet and which will in all probability lead to serious mental health problems. ▼ The most profoundly disturbing part of the 1992 directive for me as a psychotherapist is item 14 of the "Applications"; this paragraph holds up self-hatred and staying in the closet as the best way to deal with a homosexual orientation:

> An individual's sexual orientation is gen
> erally not known to others unless he pub-

licly identifies himself as having this orientation or unless some overt behavior
manifests it. As a rule, the majority of
homosexual persons who seek to lead
chaste lives do not want or see no reason
for their sexual orientation to become
public knowledge. Hence the problem of
discrimination in terms of employment,
housing, etc., does not arise.[9]

Once again the Vatican has produced a statement
that empirical evidence directly contradicts. Almost without
exception, every gay and lesbian person I know would give
anything to be able to live out of the closet. They remain in the
closet only out of fear. But the Vatican statement does not acknowledge reality and, instead, holds up the most pathological adjustment to a homosexual orientation as both the ideal
and the norm. ▼ Item 14 paraphrases a previous instruction
from the Congregation of the Religious (the Congregation in
charge of setting norms for candidates for the priesthood and
religious life) advising Bishops and heads of religious orders
to accept only those gay candidates for priesthood or the religious life whose gayness is "egodystonic," a psychological
term which implies a pathological self-hatred. They are directed to refuse any candidate whose homosexuality is "egosyntonic," that is, anyone who is a healthy and happy self-
accepting homosexual. ▼ Instructions like these lead me to
believe that Vatican officials, motivated by hubris, respond to
criticism by saying, in effect, "Don't bother us with the facts!
This is true because we say it is true! There is no room in the
Catholic Church teaching for any kind of dialogue or demo-

cratic process." ▼ **Praying over these documents as a gay Catholic theologian and therapist fully aware of the enormous destruction they will cause in the psychic life of young gay people, especially Catholics, and of the enormous amount of violence and political persecution of gay people in general they can and already have unleashed, I find myself in a profound dilemma. What kind of faith and trust can I place in a teaching authority that is clearly acting in an unloving, hateful, and destructive way?** ▼ **Certainly, the Church has the right to participate in dialogue with the rest of the human community in a search for the truth. There is no mandate from Jesus Christ, however, that gives the Church the right to create the truth by fiat. We look in vain for the humility that was once found in Church statements, such as this one from the 1966 Vatican Council:**

> **Laymen should also know that it is gen-
> erally the function of their well-formed
> Christian conscience to see that the divine
> law is inscribed in the life of the earthly
> city. From priests they may look for spir-
> itual life and nourishment. Let the layman
> not imagine, however, that his pastors
> are always such experts that to every
> problem which arises, however compli-
> cated, that they can readily give him a
> quick solution, or even that such is their
> mission. Rather, enlightened by Christian
> wisdom and giving close attention to the
> teaching authority of the Church, let the
> layman take on his own distinctive role.[10]**

My only consolation at this time lies in three profound hopes. First, I pray that the very absurdity and hateful spirit of these documents will lead the Catholic lay person to refuse to receive them and to discern spiritually the contradiction between these documents and the spirit of Jesus as portrayed in the Gospels. Second, I hope that the Church will proceed soon to call together a third Vatican council which will change radically the way authority functions in the Catholic Church. The current structure that produces documents such as the 1992 directive is rapidly undermining credibility in the Catholic magisterium, while the world desperately needs the credible moral authority of the Church. This third Vatican council, among other tasks, should create new structure that will allow a democratic process in which what the Holy Spirit is revealing in the lives of people can be heard by an enlightened hierarchy. ▼ Meanwhile, I hope that my lesbian sisters and gay brothers will be able to draw on all the good things the Church has to offer them for their health and holiness in its sacramental life, while protecting themselves against the poisons of a pathologically homophobic religion.

▼

CHAPTER 6

CREATING *the* AUTHENTIC GAY

SELF: *The* THREE-STAGE PROCESS

The Vatican view then is that the ideal life-style for gays and lesbians is to stay in the closet and lead lives devoid of any intimacy or sexual fulfillment. In sharp contrast, many other theologians, combining psychological understanding of sexual development with a deep understanding of theology, advise gays and lesbians to come out of the closet, positively accept their gayness, and open themselves to the possibility of a loving and committed sexual relationship. The Catholic theologians Evelyn and James Whitehead, for example, have a remarkable chapter called "Passages in Homosexual Holiness" in their book *Seasons of Strength: New Visions of Adult Christian Maturing*.[1] In this chapter the Whiteheads deal with what they see as the three necessary stages of coming out of the closet that gay people must undertake if they are to achieve any degree of homosexual health and holiness. The Whiteheads' understanding stands in total contradiction to the message implicit in the Vatican documents previously cited. I make use here of the Whiteheads' three-stage process to homosexual holiness to outline the program which, after twenty-five years of counseling and psychotherapy with lesbians and gays, I am convinced has the best chance to lead to health and to spiritual maturity.

The Whiteheads identify three passages in homosexual holiness: the passage into self-love, the passage into love of each other, and the passage into public witness to God's love for us. The religious symbol of passage is derived from the Israelite experience of passage from slavery in Egypt through the desert to their new homeland in Israel.[2] The central paradox of a passage is always both loss and gain; in a time of passage we become vulnerable to both personal loss and unexpected grace. Every passage begins in disorientation and the threat of loss. It matures into a second stage as we allow ourselves to fully experience and to name the loss. In the reluctant, gradual letting go of the old self and gingerly admitting in of the new self, we are losing ourselves and finding ourselves.

It is this middle part of a passage, this in-between time, that most of my clients experience as very frightening. How can we be sure that if we let go of the security of the closet there will be new selves that can survive outside the closet; especially since we constructed those closets because we thought our lives depended on it? I am reminded of the joke about the man hiking in the mountains who falls off a cliff. Fortunately he is able to catch hold of a branch which breaks his fall. Hanging there, he calls out, "Is there anyone up there?" A voice answers: "Yes, my son!" "Help me!" the man cries out. "All right, my son," the voice says, "Let go of the branch and I'll take care of you!" The man thinks for a while and then cries out, "Is there anyone else up there?" In the disorientation and darkness of a passage, we cannot see the other side, we cannot be sure, cannot control, where the journey leads. Staying in a closet is a way of trying to stay in control without needing to trust God.

John Fortunato in his gay spiritual classic *Embracing the Exile: Healing Journeys of Gay Christians* deals with the gay experience of passage under another biblical symbol, that of "Exile."[3] Using this symbol, Fortunato brings out the psychological and spiritual meaning of self-acceptance for gays. Fortunato identifies staying in the closet with the fundamental myth of our culture, the myth that happiness and fulfillment can be achieved by belonging in this world. We lesbians and gays are aware that our very existence as homosexually oriented persons makes us exiles in our heterosexist culture. If we come out of the closet we will most frequently have the painful and frightening experience of being exiles from family, friends, church, and culture. We will experience being outsiders who no longer belong.

Consequently, in Fortunato's view, many gay people strive to hide their gay identity, even from themselves, in order to be accepted. The only healthy spiritual way to deal with our exile status is for gay people to go through a process of mourning, gradually letting go of our desire to belong to and be accepted by all the structures of the heterosexist world. At the same time we must deepen our experience of belonging in the spiritual world.

This mourning process, I believe, recapitulates the ancient spiritual practice of detachment. A complete mourning process has several stages. Elizabeth Kübler-Ross has oulined five stages of mourning: denial, compromise, anger, depression, and finally acceptance.[4] Many gays and lesbians fail to complete that process. As a result they can get stuck, for example, at the denial stage, trying to live out their lives as a false self, suppressing or denying their reality as a gay person. They can try the compromise stage, e.g., marrying and clandestinely engaging in gay sex, or acting straight during the business week and going to gay bars dressed in leather on the weekend. They can also get stuck at the stage of anger or depression, becoming full of bitterness and cynicism.

But if a gay or lesbian person completes that mourning process, he or she will have already completed the detachment process from this world that most people are challenged to achieve only as they approach death. This is one reason why so many gay men with AIDS have been able to deal with impending death with extraordinary peace and tranquillity.

> What gay people have to give up is attachment to rejection and the need for people (incapable or unwilling to do so) to affirm their wholeness and lovableness. If you give up denying, fighting and wallowing in depression, you stop being stuck in the mud. Off you go, down the road. You begin to see that freedom and a sense of belonging aren't to be found in the myth at

all. They never were. You begin to understand what
Jesus meant when he said: "Mine is not a kingdom of
this world" (John 18:36).[5]

This spirit of detachment has become especially important
during this period of the AIDS crisis. By deepening their spiritual life
gays can turn what they see as the curse of gayness, the curse of being
in exile, into spiritual gold by realizing that in proportion as they are
exiles in this world, they belong ever more deeply to the kingdom of
God.

The First Passage

According to the Whiteheads the peculiar dynamic of any
passage is to be found in the mourning process, a process of loss and
discovery. "Psychologically, we grow by letting go parts of ourselves no
longer necessary for our journey; we are purified of parts of ourselves that
do not fit the future."[6] Most lesbian and gay people who undertake the
passage of coming out of the closet find that, although it is a time of
vulnerability and loss, it is also a time for potential grace. The most
moving session of the many retreats at Kirkridge that Virginia Mollen-
kott and I have given for lesbian and gay Christians has been what we
call the "fish-bowl" experience. At these meetings a self-selected group
of gay people tell the story of their journey in coming out of the closet
with its moments of terror and loss and also its moments of joy and
fulfillment. Often it is only with hindsight that we begin to recognize
the gracefulness and the presence of God in a time of passage. We experience the opportunity for extraordinary growth. We find unsuspected
strengths; we are startled by our ability to risk and to trust. From that
process we emerge not just different, but stronger. We find both new
direction and new confidence in our life.

The Whiteheads' first passage is the passage from the closet
of ignorance or denial to the light of self-acceptance. They point out that
the closet, as the starting point for the passage of coming out, is an image of a space that shares many features with a womb. It is a protective
and dark space that serves as a hiding place. It is at once secure and con-
fining. Just as an infant needs its nine months in the womb, so the av-

erage gay growing up in a homophobic, heterosexist culture needs the protection of the closet for a certain period of time. It serves as an important developmental haven which like the womb is meant eventually to be outgrown. The failure to do so can result in the stunting of psychological and spiritual growth. The process of venturing out of the secure confinement of the closet initiates a dangerous and exciting lifelong journey.

We begin the first passage when, after years of avoiding and denying the inner movements of affection and attraction to members of the same sex, we find ourselves inclined to let go of the charades we have been playing with ourselves and to befriend and accept our own sexual identities. We are invited to self-intimacy, to acknowledge and embrace the persons we are with the enduring affections, desires, and feelings which constitute our selves. It is important to realize that being gay is not just a question of performing certain kinds of sexual acts; even heterosexuals can perform those actions. It is, rather, a fundamental difference in our very essence and in our power to love!

How often I have worked as a therapist with gay or lesbian clients who have been in such terror of admitting their gayness that they come close to psychotic breakdown in the process of trying to maintain their denial. To listen to and to own the movements of affection in our own hearts places us in great jeopardy. In the midst of this passage, which is the only route to the maturing of our adult identity and vocation, we experience deep fear and doubt. Our homophobic culture and Church do all in their power to reinforce this self-denial that keeps gay people in the dark, even to themselves, by making the claim that if they do positively accept themselves and act out that acceptance they will not only experience a legitimate exile in this world, but they will be exiled as evil for all eternity in heaven. But once they make the breakthrough and are able to admit and love their gayness, the peace and joy my clients experience is overwhelming. And for the first time they have a clear understanding of who they are being called to be. They understand from their own experience what Irenaeus meant when he wrote: "The Glory of God are humans fully alive."

How do we succeed in making that passage? Not through our own resources. Whether we recognize it or not, it is a gift of God's! This first passage is a passage to self-love, and self-love is one of those actions that philosopher Maurice Blondel identified as "necessary and impossible" by human means alone.[7] Consequently, if you find yourself truly loving and accepting yourself, you have grounds to be deeply grateful to God; the gift has been given.

Self-love and acceptance are not one-time gifts; we are constantly growing toward deeper self-love and self-acceptance. We learn to be intimate with ourselves, the first form of intimacy. Insofar as we are in the closet to ourselves we are not being intimate with ourselves. We are denying our reality; we are pretending to be something we aren't; we are deliberately staying out of touch with our deepest feelings and emotions; we are not allowing ourselves to be authentic in any way. We can be thorough-going inauthentic human beings. As a result, there can be no self-intimacy. And, if there is no self-intimacy, there can be no intimacy with others.

We need, therefore, to have whatever is preventing us from really accepting and loving ourselves removed: we need to be healed in that woundedness; we need to be empowered to really love ourselves. And that is grace! God invites us to acknowledge and embrace the persons we are.

I cannot emphasize enough the value of psychotherapy with a gay-positive therapist in this process. Many of us internalized our self-hatred in early childhood. The homophobic voice that speaks within us frequently speaks with the voice of our parents. (My superego speaks with an Irish accent which I can clearly recognize as the voice of Katie, my stepmother.) As we grow up we see ourselves in our parents' eyes as in a mirror; whatever pleases them we incorporate positively into our psyche; whatever displeases them we incorporate negatively as something we hate about ourselves.

There is also what I call "the keeping mother and father good" syndrome; this syndrome leads us, whenever we come across some aspect of our parent that is not good, to try to keep the parent good by taking that badness into ourselves. As D. W. Winnicott puts it: "Every child knows that it would rather be a devil in a world ruled by a good God, than a saint in a world ruled by a devil!"[8] The result of that syndrome is that we repress all anger directed toward our parents by turning it inward and directing it toward ourselves: "I must be really bad to make Mother so angry!" We emerge from that process with a low self-image that cripples us in our effort to accept and live out a gay life.

If our psychic traumas arise in the context of the interpersonal relationship we had with parenting figures, then the cure of those traumas can take place best in the interpersonal context of "reparenting" with a gay-positive therapist. Clients gradually replace their self-condemning voices taken in from parents with new and healthy interior voices which allow the clients to accept themselves as gay and live out that positive acceptance with gratitude to God.

Many of us have erroneous psychological ideas that can unnecessarily complicate our journey. Most important, many people, including even the Whiteheads, do not fully realize that being gay is not a matter of choice.[9] Young people can't say: "Well, I can go either way!" This is simply not true! In twenty-five years of working with lesbian and gay people I have come across only one instance of pseudo-homosexuality: a young man who entered into a homosexual relationship with an adult male in order to obtain affection, but whose true orientation was heterosexual. But I have dealt with hundreds of males who have lived out lives of pseudo-heterosexuality, frequently with disastrous consequences. Psychologically we have no more choice over being gay or straight than we have over the color of our eyes.

The first passage is interior in two different senses: it takes place within the individual, and it can take place without interpersonal expression. Coming out of this closet is a private experience. It simply consists of saying, "I am gay and I love my gayness." Yet it can be a very difficult step. Interiorized self-hatred is the sin of gay people, and gay people must learn to see it that way. We are taught in a homophobic culture to interiorize our self-hatred; we need the demon of that self-hatred exorcised. We have to realize somehow or other that God loves us as we are, as gay men and lesbian women. And if we have that sense that God loves us, if that knowledge touches our hearts, we can begin to love ourselves. We can let go of all self-hatred and the desire to be something other than what we are. We can begin to genuinely love ourselves.

The Whiteheads say that those Christians who find themselves to be predominantly and enduringly homosexual must come to accept and love this most important part of themselves. It is necessary to do so. One has no choice. To stay in the closet is to despair that God can love you as you are. To refuse this passage, to turn back because of the terror of this transition is to fail in a fundamental way in your trust of God.[10]

The spiritual struggle, then, for most gays and lesbians is to achieve trust in God and in themselves. To achieve self-trust we must develop our capacity to hear what God is saying directly to us in our own experience. We must learn to trust the words of Scripture: "Yes, you love everything that exists, / and nothing that you have made disgusts you, / since, if you had hated something, you would not have made it" (Wis. 11:24).[11]

Once you begin to love yourself, you don't let yourself take abuse or be pushed around anymore. And as soon as you do that, all hell is going to break loose. Both the Church and society will accept the self-hating gay. I have already mentioned a recent Vatican document which tells us that we should choose to stay in the closet. Cardinal O'Connor was once quoted in the *New York Times* as saying that he had nothing against homosexuality as long as its practitioners saw themselves as sinful. But the moment you say: "Look, I am good! And my sexual affections and my desire to reach out and express my homosexual feelings in a sexual gesture is good. It is a way of expressing genuine human love and a healthy human love toward another human being. There is nothing wrong with it," you are in trouble.

But this trouble is good trouble. It's healthy trouble. It's the trouble that comes with growth and development. To deny the existence and the goodness of our gay affections, our desires, and our affective orientation necessarily undermines all our adult efforts to love, work, and create, and thus diminishes any positive contribution we can make in this world. I am reminded of the biblical parable about the man who buried his talents out of fear of the master (Matt. 25:14–30). Our contribution in helping this world to become one with the divine is to love. If the only way we can love is as gay persons and we, then, deny our gayness and, therefore, deny our feelings and refuse to give or receive love, we are denying God the means to enter into this world through us.

Religious maturity means nothing at all without self-awareness and self-intimacy. Without self-love we cannot fulfill the most important commandment: to love God, and one's neighbor as oneself.

If you hate yourself, you will hate your neighbor. In fact, you may be tempted to succumb to *The Boys in the Band* syndrome, hating all your gay brothers and lesbian sisters and acting out that mutual hatred in very destructive ways.[12] A gay community united by its hatred can become a diabolical force in the world. No evil can be greater than that of a closeted gay acting out his or her self-hatred toward those gays who are trying to live healthy lives out of the closet. Frequently I have the impression that this is the source of much of our problem with the Church hierarchy.

The first passage, then, is necessary. There is no escaping it, you've got to take it. You've got to freely open yourself up to God's grace. And as soon as you feel any self-condemnation, self-hatred, guilt, shame, or homophobia in yourself, you've got to see these feelings as a diabolical evil. You've got to fight them tooth and nail and pray hard for the grace to overcome them. Substitute for those negative feelings, feelings of joy and gratitude for the gift of your gayness!

How long does this passage take? Both psychological research and pastoral experience suggest that, in the past, the average gay man took about thirty-four years to come to self-acceptance. It took about thirty-four years to work through and free oneself from the homophobia of our culture and learn to be truly comfortable with oneself. I frequently have worked with men in their fifties and sixties who have still not made this passage. For people growing up gay or lesbian in recent times the amount of time varies tremendously. In fact, some teenagers today come out and seem settled in their identities while still in their late teens or early twenties.[13]

I believe that gay liberation is providing a social climate where role models and safe spaces exist, enabling many of us to come out of the closet and live fulfilled lives as gay or lesbian sooner rather than later. Certainly, being in therapy with a gay-positive therapist, attending a gay retreat or a gay-positive weekend, or belonging to a gay organization such as a gay church and attending meetings can speed up the process. It is a process; it can be a difficult one, and it is one we have to keep working at.

The length of the first passage in coming to a clear self-recognition as homosexual has both benefits as well as the more obvious difficulties. The person who has come through this passage frequently develops a very profound and dynamic spiritual life based on a powerful sense of the presence and effectiveness of God's grace. Gays who have achieved self-acceptance through this process are much more secure in their identity, more self-loving, and no longer dependent on the approval of outside agencies to affirm and accept themselves. My own experience is that as a result of this passage I have achieved with God's grace a peace and a joy in my gayness no one can take from me! I am able to celebrate my gayness as a special gift from God.

Rituals for the First Passage of Coming Out

The Whiteheads make the point that this passage of coming out to ourselves is a sacred time, a time of spiritual growth and maturity. Therefore, there should be an appropriate ritual marking this passage. "So frightened have we been of the homosexual members of our mystical body that we have ignored the graces that have accompanied the quiet interior passage to self-acceptance of so many homosexual Christians."[14] In place of any public rite of passage, the Church tends to isolate its ministry to the private, hidden, closet-like settings of the confessional or the counseling room. Rites of passage, however, by their very nature should be public events in which we acknowledge, invoke, and celebrate the action of God's grace.

This first passage is essentially private and interior. How can we protect this privacy without rendering it closeted and secretive? The Whiteheads suggest that at the present time the Church can help make this passage as public as possible by sponsoring community discussions of homosexual maturing, recognizing coming out of the closet as one of the patterned modes of grace and maturity within the Christian community. The Church should also make available and recommend a growing body of theological and pastoral writing in which this first interior passage and other graceful events in the lives of lesbian and gay members are brought to light and celebrated. I look forward to the day when the Church rethinks the sacrament of confirmation, the sacrament of maturing, which celebrates coming out of the closet, as the Apostles came out of the upper room, for mature adult Christians publicly acknowledging and affirming their faith. There should be an equivalent rite for gay Christians seeking the special grace they need to become mature and adult gay believers. Some Metropolitan Community Church communities have already experimented in designing this rite.

At the heart of the ritual of confirmation is the concept of arriving at spiritual maturity. The person being confirmed exercises the power from the Holy Spirit to be able to depend on personal experience, to discern spirits, and to depend no longer on outside authority. These are all spiritual gifts which, as we have seen, are essential to the psychic and spiritual health of gay people.

CHAPTER 7

The SECOND PASSAGE *into*

INTIMACY *with* ANOTHER

Sooner or later lesbians and gay men will experience an invitation and a challenge to share themselves with others. In the first interior passage, we are invited to a deeper acceptance and love of ourselves. In the second passage, we are led by the divine spirit, the spirit of love, into another adventure, another growth episode. We are led into a mode of presence with others where we are known for who we are. As the Whiteheads put it, "I gradually let go of the safety of not being known, the security of sexual anonymity. Strengthened by a growing comfort with myself (the grace of the first passage), I am encouraged to depart from this protective anonymity and enter the risk, the excitement, of being known as I am."[1] That very act of coming out of the closet to a friend, to a counselor, to a spiritual director, to a potential lover, is absolutely essential to our health and to our holiness.

These first two passages may occur at the same time. Yet we can distinguish them as two different challenges. The first is the struggle to achieve self-acceptance, and the second is acting on the desire to be known and loved for who we are. Until we are loved by someone who knows us completely, we will find it very difficult to believe that God loves us.

I doubt that many of you thought this way about it, but that first "trick" you ever took home from a bar, no matter how ashamed and guilty you felt about it, may have been a step toward homosexual holiness. You were sharing life, choosing life. You were choosing to be authentic and to share who you are in an honest way.

The danger of this second step lies in the rejection and humiliation that can result if we risk sharing ourselves. For this reason, it is important to be careful in choosing where you come out and whom you come out to. Choose the right time and the right person! Many of my clients have made the worst, the most self-destructive, choices in coming out. They came out where they were guaranteed total rejection and as a result took a step backward into self-hatred and self-rejection. For example, they came out to homophobic parents in a moment of anger in order to hurt them. A gay or lesbian person should consider the consequences of coming out, weigh his or her ability to face a possible negative reaction, and choose only the people who are most likely to be genuinely loving and respectful in their response.

Individuals who are coming out also need safe *communities* in which the process can take place publicly. Lesbian and gay religious communities, such as Dignity, Integrity, Metropolitan Community Churches, Affirmation, Lutherans Concerned, and the other lesbian and gay groups affiliated with all the major denominations, are essential to a healthy environment where individuals are nourished in their process of coming out. We also need straight churches which have a public policy of being inclusive. If we are able to come out first within the confines of a secure community, our self-love and self-esteem are strengthened and our interiorized homophobia overcome.

The delay of this second passage of intimacy, as with the first, can lead to serious problems. If you keep putting off the coming out process until you are forty or fifty years old, it may become increasingly more difficult. For example, your closest friends and colleagues may feel angry or betrayed that you have hidden your sexual orientation, such an important part of yourself, from them. They may demand, "Why didn't you share this with me before? Why didn't you trust me enough to share this? Why did you hold it back?" It is important not to let fear of their anger hold you back, but to give everyone—your friends, your family, your community, yourself, and God—a chance to love you for who you really are.

Once you let your family and friends know that you are gay, they will most likely go through a mourning process. If your parents have always envisioned themselves as grandparents and looked forward to playing with the grandchildren you would bring them, they may feel especially cheated. It may take some time before they can readjust to who you are. And they may express rejection or anger or bitterness toward you which will swing back and forth into self-accusation and self-condemnation: "Where did I go wrong in raising you?" Parents need to learn that they are not responsible for the homosexual orientation of their child. But they can play an important role in determining whether or not that child grows up happy and healthy. If a child senses that parental love for him or her is a conditional love, conditioned on the child's conformity to the parents' needs, he or she may be less than well-adjusted.[2]

Parents must also reexamine all the cultural stereotypes of homosexuality in order to readjust their understanding of homosexuality to fit into the image of the daughter or son they love: "You can't be gay! I never saw you in women's clothing!" Parents who come from a strong religious background may face the especially difficult task of overcoming their fear that their child's homosexuality is a fatal flaw that will cut him or her off from God's love and mercy. Before they can accept their gay children, parents also will have to go through all the steps of mourning that their children went through in order to accept themselves. They will experience denial. "It can't be true," a parent may say. "Didn't you have a girlfriend in high school?" Or they ask for compromise: "Couldn't you get married anyhow and have a boyfriend (or a girlfriend) on the side?"

Given the years it usually takes us to accept our sexuality, we should be willing to give our parents the time they need to be reconciled with our gayness. Give them room to go through all the stages of mourning and pray that God's grace will give them the strength to complete that process. The vast majority will come through; sooner or later they will accept, love, and respect a gay son or lesbian daughter.

No one wants to go through life saying to himself or herself: If they really knew who I am, they would not love me! The feeling that one must remain hidden to secure love works like a sickness in the soul. And if we go through life with that feeling, we have failed in a fundamental way to learn to trust the goodness and love of our parents or friends. Coming out of the closet to someone we love is a courageous act of trust and love. Pray to God for the courage to be able to make that act of love.

A common mistake among gays is to plunge into interpersonal intimacy without doing the first step, the interior passage of self-acceptance. A lot of people try to substitute step two for step one, and it seldom works. This tendency, I believe, is the main problem with gay political organizations. We announce ourselves, "I'm gay! I'm here to stay! I'm not going away!" in the hope that, if the public accepts us and loves us, we may be able to accept and love ourselves. If we still unconsciously hate ourselves and our sexuality, we will be tempted to make this announcement in an angry way to precisely the wrong people (e.g., to Cardinal O'Connor at high mass). When this bid for acceptance inevitably fails, we have created our own self-defeating situation. It is very important, then, to follow these steps in the right order. Deal in a very private way and in very intimate relationships with your self-acceptance first.

Another mistaken approach to the second passage is through the busy, if not frenzied, activity of the narcissistic person. Narcissistic persons are trapped by their own interior needs and cannot reach out and achieve authentic intimacy with others. Revealing themselves to others again and again, hoping through that process to learn who they are, having side-stepped the earlier passage, and lacking confidence and comfort with themselves, narcissistic persons deal in facile self-revelation and instant intimacy. But this activity of self-disclosure and sharing, which at first appears to be the work of the second passage, never takes hold. The grace of this passage, a sustained, enduring relationship with somebody, never occurs because such persons do not love themselves. The notorious one-night-stand phenomenon in gay male circles is an example of such narcissism. People who have one-night stands but are incapable of intimacy frequently act this way because they do not love themselves. In fact, they despise themselves for compulsively needing to use people as sexual objects. After having sex, they can't wait to get out of there; they run for the door tearing up their sexual partner's telephone number on the way out. They never want to see their sexual partner again because the encounter represents what they hate and fear most about themselves. And if they are good Catholic members of Courage, they go to confession, tell Father that they were drunk, that they fell into temptation and hate what they did, and they beg God for forgiveness. But this behavior does not require courage. All it requires is a willingness to make a habit of self-hatred.

Having sex with hundreds of people will not necessarily do anything to help you accept yourself. On the contrary, it may deepen your self-hatred; every single act can deepen the self-hatred. There is only one way to come through to self-love and that is to sense that God loves us as we are and that our sexual expression in an intimate and loving context does not separate us from that divine love but unites us ever more deeply with it. That is grace, and it is this grace that heals the wound of self-hatred. Then, knowing that we are lovable, we can reach out in genuine human love to other human beings. We can enjoy sexual intimacy as a positive expression of our loving desire to give and receive pleasure from other adults.

Whenever one of my clients tells me, "I met someone last night at the gay bar. We went home together and made out, and I think this is the person I want to share life with!" I always ask, "Did he ever have any other relationship? Does he really like himself?" Unless both you and your partner are secure in yourselves, you could be heading for real trouble. Homophobia or self-hatred of one's gayness has been so prevalent in the gay community that it is the primary impediment to genuine intimacy for lesbian and gay couples.

This second passage has been described as a passage into intimacy. By intimacy is meant the psychological and spiritual resources which allow us to sustain the ambiguities, the excitement, and the strain of being up close to another human being. It is often very difficult to be intimate with someone because of the enormous strain such a relationship puts on our psychological resources. It takes a reasonably healthy person to be able to be intimate; you are inviting another whole world into your world and trying to adjust with all the give and take involved. Even heterosexuals, with all the advantages they enjoy, are finding the passage into intimacy extremely difficult. One-half of heterosexual unions end in divorce. Unless you have learned to love yourself as gay, the strains and ambiguities of intimacy are going to lead to rage and anger, which will cause the relationship to fail.

This passage is necessary for most homosexuals today precisely because it is so difficult to sustain friendships and working relationships while keeping in the closet. Life can be so unhappy for many lesbians and gays because they feel that they are never genuine, that they are always playing a role. The acceptance they feel from their fellow workers or church members is based on a lie. They may fear that the only time they will ever come out of the closet is at the moment of death. Then the real gay man or lesbian will stand face to face with God and, of course, that will have to be a moment of sheer terror. If you have never risked it, never risked being yourself, never risked an authentic love, then you will have to do so on your deathbed. Consequently, you cannot look forward to death with peace, trust, and hope. The solution is to take the risk now!

Decisions about sexual or genital expressions of intimacy are separable from this movement into intimacy. Whether Christian adults choose a celibate or sexually active life-style, they still must face this passage. In the deepest sense of the word, intimacy is not optional; to know God, you must love. If you never let yourself love with a gay love, you will never (barring a miracle of God's grace) know God intimately in this life! As gay people, the natural way for us to know God's love is through gay love. This is one reason why the policy of many religious orders, who will accept gay candidates only as long as they keep their gayness a private secret, is so reprehensible.

The Role of the Church

How can the Church facilitate this passage for its gay and lesbian members? Currently, psychotherapy and spiritual direction are the catalysts for this passage for many people. The Church should provide gay-positive counseling or therapy. If, however, the confessional or the therapy sessions are still viewed as sickness- or sin-oriented exchanges between patient and therapist or priest and penitent, then these sessions can only lead the gay person deeper into his or her pathology.

Instead we gay people need a setting for a developmentally oriented exchange between the adult patient and the therapist or the adult Christian and a religious guide. We need a place where we are free without judgment or condemnation to talk about our deepest spiritual life, our longings, our fears, and our needs, and to get those needs authenticated in a deep exchange between our real self and the real self of the other person. Over the past twenty years organizations and churches such as Dignity, Integrity, Metropolitan Community Church, the gay synagogue, and the many open, gay-positive congregations and churches in the Protestant churches have offered an explicitly religious context for lesbian or gay Christians or Jews to meet each other and to come out of the closet within a safe and accepting community of love. Also encouraging has been the increase in the number of retreats available for homosexuals as another social context where this passage can take place.[3]

The role of churches in this passage is dual: to protect and to predict. Through gay religious organizations, through retreats and other support groups, the believing community protects gay and lesbian people who are struggling to let themselves be and to develop a style of intimacy at once gay and religious. These church-supported groups protect individuals from culture's scorn, and they protect them from isolation, from having to experience this difficult transition alone.

These church groups also have the function of predicting the outcome of the passage. Here the accumulated wisdom of the community ministers to an individual's experience: "This passage, which you experience as unique and special, has happened before. God is at work here!" The community witnesses to what God is about and assures us that we will come through. God is stripping us of a once necessary anonymity and calling us to share ourselves with others. In its rites a community encourages us to let go and to trust this process of purification and growth. The contribution of the community is crucial because our individual experiences are so limited. If I let go of part of myself, how can I trust that this will lead to a better, more mature way of living? This is a question my religious community is able to, or should be able to, answer.

We gay people have a desperate need to understand our lives and experience in the light of Scripture. We have a need to hear the story of others who have undertaken the gay spiritual journey with its unique perils and opportunities. One of the great tragedies of gay people in the past has been their enforced isolation from one another and their inability to pass on a history and a legacy to younger generations.

As Tom Clarke, S.J., in *Tracing the Spirit: Communities, Social Action, and Theological Reflection,* says: "To be deprived of one's story is the most ruthless form of oppression. Individuals, groups, people who society through racism, sexism, classism [and heterosexism] has denied ownership of a distinctive story will inevitably be tempted to despair of themselves."[4] One of the most serious obstacles to healthy spiritual liberation for gays and lesbians has been the Church itself. A recent example is the effort of the Roman Catholic hierarchy to drive Dignity out of the Church and to keep its gay members isolated or bound together in self-hatred in organizations such as Courage.

As the Whiteheads observe, an "ungraceful" part of our recent religious history has been the community's denial of homosexual maturing. With such a denial, the believing community forfeits its role of protecting and predicting this pattern of religious growth, and homosexual Christian maturity remains closeted, hidden. Thus "darkened," it cannot perform its generative function: to witness to the next generation the shape of this Christian journey with both its perils and its graces.[5]

CHAPTER 8

A PUBLIC PASSAGE

Some gay and lesbian people reach a third passage in their life journey; this passage is a call to be recognized as both homosexual and religious persons in the public world. Some gays are called to play a prophetic role in trying to achieve justice for the lesbian and gay community through political organizations, gay rights groups. Others are called to a service role in the gay community through organizations such as the Gay Men's Health Crisis, Senior Action in a Gay Environment, and the Lesbian and Gay Community Center.

This public passage is religious when it includes coming out precisely as a gay person and a person of religious faith. The Whiteheads, speaking in the Christian tradition, stress that while the first two passages cannot be ignored but must be taken by all gays, this third public passage need not be taken by all homosexual Christians.[1] They stress the perils that are attached to any public acknowledgment of oneself as gay. The probability of recriminations from both society and church, the loss of one's job, for example, or expulsion from the priesthood or religious life, are very real. Most Christians who have matured through the first passage of self-acceptance and have risked the second passage of intimacy with a few others continue to grow in the ways of Christ without coming out publicly.

Many homosexuals are extraordinarily attracted to service roles in the human community. Gays are frequently called to a generative role where they can give to the community at large the love and affection that most heterosexuals reserve for their children. Many homosexuals feel called to positions as teachers, social workers, hospital orderlies and nurses, student counselors, psychologists, and clergypersons—in fact, to any occupation where they can be of direct service to their fellow humans. It is my belief that the presence of the lesbian and gay community within the human community is essential to its human development. Gays are the oil that keeps the whole machine running smoothly. This is so true that if, somehow, suddenly there were no gay people, the human community would be in serious jeopardy.[2]

I believe that at this moment in history God is calling many of us to a public witness to the compatibility of being lesbian or gay and religious persons of deep faith. Like the rich young man in the gospel who is called by Jesus to sell all his possessions, give the money to the poor, and enter into an intimate discipleship with Jesus (Matt. 19:16–22), we also are in danger of fearing that call and turning away. Until we hear and respond to the call to deeper intimacy with God and with Jesus, there is interior disquiet; the moment we respond positively there is an experience of deep peace and joy and the willingness "to rejoice because we have been found worthy to suffer something for the sake of Christ." I speak here from my own experience. When I was offered the choice to give up my public ministry to lesbians and gays or to be dismissed from the Society of Jesus, which had been my family and my security for over forty years, I knew which choice God was calling me to! But I was afraid that the loss of my relationship with the Jesuits would lead to a deep depression and debilitating sorrow. On the contrary, after my final conversation with the Jesuit General in which it was decided that I would be dismissed from the Jesuits, I left that room filled with joy and peace and a deeper certitude that what I was doing was the will of God for me. Greater joy than that no one can have!

One must be careful about the motive which leads one to make a public witness. All of us have some desire to be in the limelight, to be seen and recognized. If this is our only motive, our public witness will probably be counterproductive. But many of us also have a more positive reason, the motive Erik Erikson calls "generativity": the impulse, felt with special urgency in mid-life, to care for and contribute to the next generation.

This virtuous instinct will lead many lesbian and gay Christians to come out publicly. As the Whiteheads say, "In so doing, their life and vocation become a public witness of homosexual and Christian maturing and a gift to the next generation."[3] Such a life provides for both homosexual and heterosexual Christians an image of what it is to be mature as Christian and as gay. Such a witness is generative, since it provides a publicly observable model of homosexual Christian life. Where there once was a void, patterns of homosexual maturing begin to appear. It becomes publicly imaginable to be both homosexual and a mature Christian.

As the Whiteheads observe, many believers have known for a long time that it is possible to be both homosexual and a Christian believer. They have heard what God is saying to them from their personal experience. But that information has not been publicly available; it has not been part of the Christian church's social imagination. In fact, the Christian church is fighting hard to prevent it from becoming such! Closeted lives, however holy, cannot provide images and models of religious maturing for others; a certain public exposure and light is required for this virtue of generativity to have its effect.

An extraordinary example of this witness is Bishop Otis Charles's recent choice to come out of the closet after his retirement as dean of the Episcopal Divinity School in Cambridge, Massachusetts. In an open letter to his fellow bishops, Bishop Charles wrote,

> *I have promised myself that I will not remain silent, invisible, unknown. After all is said and done, the choice for me is not whether or not I am a gay man, but whether or not I am honest about who I am with myself and others. I would hope that I might be remembered for helping to create a world in which the church is seriously addressing the experience of gay people in ways that strengthen the confidence and self-*

esteem of individuals who are discovering their gayness
in a world that is framed by a heterosexual construct.[4]

The Spirit is calling all of us to a new understanding and experience of inclusion, the Bishop wrote. "I believe that as gay men and lesbians speak openly, telling the stories of their lives, the community of faith is strengthened." By coming out Bishop Charles acknowledges that new opportunities will be open to him to share his story. He is delighted that he might be able to help families, especially parents with gay children. "I would like to focus on a transformation of consciousness to free parents to see that their children may be different and that there's nothing wrong with that."

CHAPTER 9

COMING OUT *through* a PUBLIC RITE *of* COVENANTED UNION

When I published *The Church and the Homosexual*, one of the chapters Church censors demanded I suppress in order to receive the *imprimi potest*, the official approval to publish, was the chapter on gay marriages. At this time, rather than gay marriage or gay union, I prefer to use the term lesbian or gay covenanted union. I prefer this terminology because marriage is derived from a French root referring to husband, *mari*, and "union" speaks only of the fusion of two partners. It can be understood as one losing his or her identity and assuming the identity of the other person, as it traditionally did in heterosexual unions, complete to the woman's losing her name. Rather than view the relationship as some kind of complete merging or blending as "union" alone might suggest, the term "covenanted union" encourages us to see a give-and-receive relationship that seeks, with the help of God, the fulfillment of two individuals. It is a "meeting of souls, souls which although eternally separate, can grow into harmony such as no other human relationship can make possible."[1]

It is with great joy that I now have the freedom publicly to record and celebrate this rite as one of the most powerful witnesses to the goodness and the holiness of gay love. During the past year I had the privilege of being invited to preside at two covenanted unions; the first was for two gay friends in the metropolitan New York area and the second was for two lesbian friends in upstate New York. In both cases all the parties involved had done a remarkably good job of making the first two passages of self-acceptance and coming out to others. I also had the privilege of being present in Pullam Baptist Church in Raleigh, North Carolina, when that church chose to celebrate a covenanted union of two gay men in the sanctuary. What was surprising and hopeful about that event was that, after long and public debate, three-quarters of the church's straight congregation approved the ceremony. In every instance, these covenantal unions were occasions of deep spiritual blessings and great peace and joy. They were transformative not only for the couple involved but for the whole community of family and friends that took part in the ritual.

I have a firm conviction that God is just as much present and involved in a loving gay Christian relationship as God is in a straight one. Again, Genesis (2:18) tells us: "It is not good that a human remain alone. Every human has need of a companion of his or her own kind!"[2] This divine purpose of companionship can be fulfilled in a gay relationship just as well as in a straight one. In fact, some people would argue that the equality that is more often recognized between gay partners makes them more capable of fulfilling that function.

From the moment the Catholic Church granted the morality of the rhythm method as a natural form of birth control for straight couples and justified sexual activity as still fulfilling what Vatican II referred to as "the equally primary aims of mutual love and fulfillment," there was a serious reason to reconsider the position that all homosexual activities are necessarily wrong on the ground that they cannot lead to procreation. In a passage in the Papal encyclical *Casti Connubii*, the mutual love between the partners is recognized in its own right as the "primary purpose and meaning of matrimony."

> *The mutual inward molding of the partners, this de-*
> *termined effort to perfect each other, can in a very real*
> *sense . . . be said to be the chief reason and purpose*
> *of matrimony, provided matrimony be looked at not in*

the restricted sense as instituted for the proper concep-
tion and education of children, but more widely as the
blending of life as a whole and the mutual inter-
change and sharing thereof.[3]

As Daniel Maguire, a noted Christian ethicist, pointed out in his article "The Morality of Homosexual Marriage," "Erotic desire is deeply interwoven into the human desire and need for closeness and for trusting relationships. The desire for a significant other with whom we are uniquely conjoined is not a heterosexual but a basic human desire. The programmatic exclusion of gay persons from the multiple benefits of erotic attraction, which often opens the way to such a union, is arbitrary, harmful, cruel, and therefore sinful."[4]

Gay and lesbian Christians should be aware that in requesting the right to a rite of covenantal union in the Church, we are only reclaiming what is an ancient tradition in the Church. John Boswell has done extensive research on the history of gay ceremonies of covenanted union and has found hundreds of lectionary services for holy unions or marriages for gay persons in ancient Church documents going back as far as the third century. Boswell traces a fifteen-hundred-year period in Church history in which the Church blessed lesbian and gay relationships. My favorite was a special blessed bonding of Irish warriors before they went into combat together.

Boswell points out that heterosexual marriages were not considered sacramental unions until as late as the thirteenth century. Most straight marriages were seen as a civil contract in which one bought a wife. "Romantic love had never been a part of the Catholic heterosexual tradition. Up until the 11th century people would not have thought of looking for love in marriage. . . . Marriage was based on respect, on procreation and on family alliance."[5]

Boswell traces the origins of the first church-sponsored heterosexual wedding ceremonies which celebrate romantic love between the partners as having been borrowed from the gay ceremonies for the making of "spiritual brotherhood" between two men; terms that Boswell points out should not be taken to mean nonromantic or necessarily nonsexual.

In most of these ceremonies there was a retelling from the

Acts of the Martyrs of the martyrdom of Bacchus and Serge. They were soldiers in the Roman army in the late third or early fourth century, very highly placed, great favorites of the pagan Roman emperor. They are called in their official Greek biography "erosti" which means gay lovers. They were denounced to the emperor for being Christian, so he asked them, as a sign of their loyalty to him, to sacrifice to pagan gods. They refused to do that. They said that they were loyal servants, but that their loyalty did not involve denying the one true God. The emperor went into a rage and ordered their belts cut off, their tunics and all other military garb removed, the gold torques taken from around their necks, and women's clothing placed on them.

To disgrace them, the emperor ordered them to be paraded through the middle of Rome to the palace wearing women's clothing and heavy chains. As they were paraded through the city, instead of feeling disgrace, they chanted together: "Yea, though we walk through the valley of the shadow of death, we will fear no evil, Lord, because denying ungodliness and worldly lusts, we have put off the form of the old man and we rejoice in you naked because you have clothed us with the garment of salvation; you have covered us with the robe of righteousness; and you have decked us as brides with women's gowns and joined us together one to the other for you through our faithfulness."[6]

Serge and Bacchus were then subjected to horrible tortures. Bacchus finally died and Serge wavered in his faith, weeping and crying out: "Oh, my other half, never again will we sing together the psalms we used to sing. Unyoked from me you have gone to heaven and left me alone here on earth, lonely and disconsolate." Then Bacchus appeared to Serge radiantly beautiful and said: "Why do you mourn and grieve, beloved? I have been taken from you bodily, but in the bond of our love I am with you still. Hurry now, so that through good and perfect fidelity you may be worthy to earn me as the reward of the race, for my crown of justice is you."

The first time I read this account, shivers ran down my spine. In the monasteries and convents of old, two gay men or two lesbian women would read this account and believe that their love for each other was a good and holy human love that would exist not only in this world, but would actually continue to exist for all eternity in the next. It was this concept of the basis for marriage as the genuine love between two humans as equal that gradually led to the heterosexual sacrament of marriage. The very formulas for gay and lesbian unions were the ones first used in church marriages of heterosexuals.

Why have a public Christian ceremony? Usually the individuals involved are looking for at least three things: affirmation, celebration, and symbolization of their relationship. The primary reason for a Christian ceremony as such should be your faith in the God which Christian tradition professes. "Whoever fails to love does not know God, because God is love!" (1 John 4:7–8). At the heart of a Christian ceremony of covenanted union is the self-giving of each mate to God, an invitation and openness to and declaration of God's loving presence in each of their lives. It is a making and preserving of a relationship of trust with this God who is the source of your love and who helps you to discover the divine course of your relationship. A wonderful attribute of a Christian ceremony is that it allows the gay couple to experience, to feel, and to know that they are within the full bonds of God's grace.

The ceremony allows the couple to declare to the world their love for each other and invite the world to come and see their shared love. In so doing, the couple strengthen each other, build each other up with an unabashed declaration of love. It can also produce a new spiritual awareness and a new understanding of who they are as a couple.

Not only do you affirm your love for each other in the act of a public ceremony, but you, along with the witnesses, also send out a message to society that what you are doing is right and just. It allows you to see, also, that others are invested in your relationship. As you become bonded in the eyes of a community which you hold dear, those of your friends and family, any discussion of a breakup will carry with it a heightened awareness of the gravity of the separation. By the power of the ritual the couple become united emotionally not only with each other but with the community as well. This can provide the foundation to see the couple through difficult times and provide "landmarks of remembrance and hope" during times of crisis.

If more gays and lesbians were to celebrate their unions, our society would awaken to the fact that sincere, committed relationships are not foreign to the gay community, but are, instead, rather common. As more people witness our ceremonies, society would begin to realize that the level of integrity in gay relationships is no less than that in straight relationships. Lawmakers might begin to understand that their refusal to recognize our relationships legally is completely unjust. Our ceremonies could fight the prejudice which maintains that we, as gay people, do not merit the rights afforded to nongay couples because we do not take our relationships seriously. We do not live isolated lives; our lives happen in the context of community. Our ceremonies help to insure that our community is more than just merely accommodating, but truly affirming and supportive.

The Whiteheads make the interesting observation that the Christian Church as an institution is also in a process of gradually "coming out."[7] That coming out process is at various stages of maturity in different denominations. We have seen over the past year many denominations publicly debating the feasibility of ordaining gay clergy in an open relationship. Many churches have adopted open door policies for gays and lesbians, accepting them as equal members of the congregation. Many dioceses of the American Catholic Church have made sensitive pastoral moves, acknowledging their gay members. Many have established special "task forces" concerned with ministry to lesbian and gay Catholics. In acknowledging the existence of and then creating public space for homosexual Catholics to stand in the community, the Church facilitates this third, public passage. As the Whiteheads observe, in doing this the Church senses, though not without some anxiety and self-doubt, that it is these maturing lesbian and gay Christians who will witness to believers the shape of homosexual holiness. However, for every positive step the American Church takes in its pastoral sensitivity to the needs of gay Catholics, the latest missive from Rome seems to send the American Church reeling backward two steps. Despite this opposition recent surveys show that over 84 percent of lay Catholics support gay rights and a greater acceptance of gay members on the part of the Church.

This is a wonderful time to be gay and Christian! How many of our gay ancestors who lived necessarily closeted, secretive lives would have rejoiced to have had one iota of the freedom we have to live out of the closet, to come together as Christians in worship and prayer, to be able to live openly in a gay relationship? My heart is continually filled with joyful gratitude to God for this blessing both for myself and my partner, Charlie, and for all my gay brothers and sisters.

PART 3

TWELVE-STEP
SPIRITUALITY

INTRODUCTION
A MEANS *of* LIBERATION *for*
LESBIANS *and* GAY MEN

In this part I will deal with the liberating power of twelve-step spirituality and its usefulness to lesbians and gay men, as well as the role gay men and lesbians can play in bringing together the masculine and feminine versions of the twelve-step process. During the twentieth century, in my opinion, the single most important development in North American spirituality has been that generated by Alcoholics Anonymous. More than a million alcoholics meet regularly in A.A. groups. They pray and meditate together, and provide mutual support as they struggle to stay sober. And they have found this program to be the most powerful tool of which they are aware to achieve liberation from addiction. ▼ In fact, I believe that the twelve-step process is the most powerful spiritual liberation process in the world today. I do not think anything equals its effectiveness among the world's great religions. We Americans have reason to be proud of that, since it was in the United States that this process came into being. At present twelve-step spiritual groups are spreading all over the world. It is at the same time the most powerful ecumenical movement among Christian denominations. ▼ Bill Wilson, the co-founder of A.A., once said that A. A. is "the story of how, under God's grace, an unsuspected strength has arisen out of a great weakness."[1] A.A. insists that its program is spiritual, not religious. For A.A. members, spirituality unites, religion divides. "Each of us," according to the Al-Anon handbook (the association for families and friends of alcoholics) "must find our way to heaven and the Al-Anon teachings reinforce our faith in the way we choose to worship, whatever it may be."[2] ▼ Twelve-step spirituality, as it developed within A.A., is a pragmatic spiritual program aimed at liberation from addiction, and it corresponds to the autonomous spiritual ideals of this book. It is a spirituality based on personal experience and discernment. Twelve-step spiritual groups have no hierarchy. By sharing their own direct experience of being helped by "the higher power" to overcome their addiction, members support each other in the spiritual quest for empowerment and liberation. ▼ Twelve-step programs are essentially American in their democratic spirit. They do not demand any esoteric practice of meditation techniques or extraordinary knowledge of "mind sciences." This spirituality is immediately open to everyone regardless of their degree of education or spiritual development. ▼ Twelve-step spiritual groups have sprung up in hundreds of different forms, for example, Sexaholics Anonymous, Narcotics Anonymous, Gamblers Anonymous, etc. It is my contention that the twelve-step program has a universal application for all of us and that its practice can

be a special help to those of us who are gay or lesbian. ▼
Each one of us is addicted to something, for addiction is a universal human condition. The first sign of addiction is compulsivity and lack of freedom and choice. I am addicted to all those behaviors over which I do not have control. For most gay people, having a strong and healthy ego is, I believe, essential to having a healthy and mature spiritual life. Addictions are extremely destructive to our mental health and self-image. Only when I have a secure self-identity can I begin the spiritual process of freely letting go of addiction in order to become one with the transcendent spirit of God. By freeing us from addiction and self-destruction, the twelve-step program can give us back our freedom, restore our healthy self-image, and prepare the way for spiritual development. ▼ Gerald May argues that all sin is a form of addiction, or idolatry.[3] We are trying to find the meaning and fulfillment of our lives in this world. With the help of a twelve-step spiritual process we can get in touch with the higher power and thus free ourself from our addiction. As soon as we are free, we will come in touch once again with a deep longing. Even if we are not aware of it, it is a longing for union with the divine because at the heart of every human there is a longing for intimate union with nothing less than God. ▼ We can be addicted in any number of ways—to alcohol, narcotics, pleasure, honors, wealth, the desire for approval, and a thousand other things. Gays and lesbians, as we have seen, can be addicted to hiding in the closet and to the myth of belonging in this world and the need of approval of others. So all of us stand in need of the liberation that the practice of twelve-step spirituality can help provide. Ideally that spiritual practice should take place in a group setting. However, since that is not always possible, I think that the steps can also

be effective when they are used in private, personal prayer.
The first three steps of the program are to acknowledge our powerlessness over our attachments,
to acknowledge a "higher power" who can
empower us, and to ask that "higher
power" for help. These are, I believe, essential steps in every
human's journey toward
intimacy with God.

▼

CHAPTER 10

INTIMACY *with* GOD

Intimacy with God is a gift given by God. In all spiritualities, there is an implicit effort to deepen our intimacy with God. To understand what this drive toward intimacy means, there are two questions to ask: What does it mean to be intimate with anybody? What are the special issues involved in being intimate with God? Everyone has some grasp of the answer to the first question in terms of the deepest human intimacies they have known.

In psychotherapy, there are two basic ways to understand the dynamics of the human psyche, two basic theses that underlie clinical practice. The first is the Freudian thesis that all human striving is for pleasure; we *cathect* objects, other human beings for the most part, because they give us pleasure. The end, then, is pleasure and in that theory, the means is the other person. My experience has led me to conclude that this theory distorts the nature of the drive in the human psyche.

The second, the theory of *object relations*, holds that the ultimate drive of the human psyche, that which is our ultimate reality, is a drive toward intimacy with other humans.[1] Intimacy means being really close to someone, to be free to let down our guard and our defenses and to let someone into our lives, into our hearts, and to share deeply with them. Having achieved intimacy we know pleasure. So pleasure is the result of intimacy and intimacy is the end, the purpose of the drive. In fact, according to this school, all striving to use others as sexual objects for selfish pleasure represents a psychopathological breakdown of the drive toward intimacy of the human spirit; a breakdown which frequently has its origin in despair of being able to achieve intimacy. I find this explanation of the human spirit much more compelling.

The root of the English word "intimacy" is derived from the Latin word *intimus*, meaning the inmost (as against the superficial or the external). To be intimate with anybody means not only to let your guard and your defenses down, it also means to be able to share what is inside you, what is deepest in yourself, fearlessly with another person and allow yourself to become vulnerable to that person.

The second Latin root of the word is *timor* or fear; to be intimate means to be without fear. It means to be able to share your feelings, your strongest and deepest feelings. The strands of all of our feelings are intermingled. If you are going to try to be intimate with somebody, you've got to be ready to experience all your feelings, the negative as well as the positive. You must be prepared to experience anger with someone with whom you wish to be intimate. You've got to be ready to be angry and to risk communicating your anger, to be powerful in your anger and expect to be heard. This is the exact opposite of the expectation of someone who envisions intimacy as symbiosis, that is, losing your identity in the other so that you can never experience anger.

You will also experience very deep fear, if you are going to open yourself to intimacy with another. *What will this cost me? Will I lose my independence and even my identity? If I become truly vulnerable to this person, how will I stand the pain of loss when he or she leaves me? And if my self-image is low, I will be certain that sooner or later he or she will realize what a loser I am and leave me.*

There is also enormous fear involved in moving toward intimacy with God. There is an insightful prayer in one of the Sunday collects which reads, "Lord! Remove the blindness that cannot know you; relieve the fear that hides me from your face!"[2] I've made that prayer my own for much of my life. I need the grace to be able to get rid of some of the blindness that results from my unconscious transferences to

God that distort God's reality, and also some of the fear that prevents me from moving into a deeper and more trusting intimacy.

The same blindness and fear that is operative in my relationship with God also prevents me from moving into a deeper intimacy with others and myself. All three intimacies go together. If you make any progress in any one of them, you also make progress in the other two. If you become more intimate with yourself and enter into a deeper knowledge and acceptance of yourself, you are at the same time more open to intimacy with your fellow humans and more open to intimacy with God.

God and the Twelve-Step Program

Ultimately, the drive of the human psyche is toward intimacy with God Herself or Himself. We are on a pilgrimage, a journey. My personal image is that our psyche is like a river flowing downstream toward the sea. That river is the divine energy that is at the core of my own psyche and my ego is floating down that river hopefully toward that final merging with the sea. I visualize every form of addiction as a side eddy which takes me out of the mainstream. To be freed from that addiction is to move back into the mainstream toward that ultimate intimacy with God, which we get touches of in deep human intimacy.

I believe that at the moment of death, I will come face to face with God Him/Herself, with a God who is love. And if I have chosen to love, I will be home, just as the river comes to the sea and becomes part of the sea without losing its unique identity. So the primary question in this life is how to unite our spirits with the divine spirit.

As Sebastian Moore puts it in his extraordinary book *Jesus: The Liberator of Desire*, the message of Jesus was not to deny our desires, to push them down, but on the contrary to *attend* to them, to ask of them, "What *do* I want?" It is only by attending to the answers that we begin to learn the difference between the compulsive, unfree, addictive movements that go by the name of desire and the *élan vital* in us of which these movements are the arrest, the dead-ending. Then we begin to see the difference between the desire of the ego to stay where it is and simply repeat past satisfactions, and the desire that can say, "I want to want more."

What we learn from the cross is the difference between liberation from *desire (the latter equated with the insatiable self-promoting ego) and the liberation of desire from the chains of my customary way of being myself. Two contrary views of asceticism present themselves here. The conventional view is that it means denying ourselves things we want. A more discerning and disconcerting view is that it means dropping things we no longer want, admitting to ourselves we no longer want them, and thus giving our journey, our story, a chance to move on—to which our Pauline "old Self" puts up a far greater resistance than to the seemingly self-afflicting deprivations that often minister to the ego.[3]*

But who is this God with whom we are seeking intimacy? In the earliest formulation of the wording of the second step, the words "God, as you understand him" were substituted for the word "God." Still later, the phrase "the higher power" was substituted. I believe there were two major reasons for this change. For many who come from a Christian background the word "God" carries with it connotations of a God of fear, who is part of the problem and not of the solution. A major part of the liberation that twelve-step spirituality accomplishes is liberation from an understanding of the Christian God as a judgmental God of fear and the discovery of the God of love. Another factor was the need to make twelve-step spirituality available to those who do not share the Christian understanding of God.

The first step reads: "We admit that we are powerless over alcohol, that our lives have become unmanageable."[4] This realization, like any spiritual change, does not occur overnight. In the tradition of A.A. there is the expression: "Work the steps." You do not just accept the twelve steps and then finish. Instead you realize and experience the meaning of each step over and over again in a deeper and deeper way. Every time you think you have got it, the next day it still has to be done all over again.

Let me share two expressions of this insight of the first step from other spiritual traditions that I find very enlightening. The first is from the writings of the philosopher Maurice Blondel. *"Spiritual life,"* Blondel writes, *"begins when we go into ourselves until we reach that point in ourselves where that which is from ourselves ceases and yet there is more."*[5] Blondel is saying in a philosophical mode exactly what the first of the twelve steps teaches. Spiritual life is the life of the divine Spirit dwelling within us. We tap into that source of power coming from divine life when we move deeply into ourselves until we reach the point where that which comes from our finite ego ceases. Yet there is more energy in there; it is in us but not from us. To tap into that energy means letting go of control, recognizing the limits of our controlling ego. All of the world's great religions recognize that the spiritual journey somehow involves letting go of the illusion of our controlling ego in order to experience an energy that goes beyond the limits of our ego.

The great mystic Teresa of Avila expresses the same insight with these words: *"The journey to God is also a journey to the self. It is an inward journey to God which is at the same time a movement into self knowledge. Union with God at the center involves the fullest possible possession of your own life."* St. Teresa believed that the only way to come into full possession of our own lives was to open ourselves up to the Spirit of God.

Step two of the twelve steps reads: "We came to believe that there is a power greater than ourselves which can restore us to sanity." Notice the great paradox in the wording of this step; that power I will turn to is greater than me and over against me. It is not me—it somehow transcends me. Yet I discover it from within myself. One of the great problems of twelve steps is that it traditionally envisioned the higher power as totally transcendent, so that God is imaged as having a kind of patriarchal power over us. This image of God misses the Christian understanding of God as Spirit dwelling in our hearts.

Sanity is ultimately three things: the ability to work, play, and love. What we are looking for through the twelve steps is to be empowered to work, play, and love in the presence of God. "The glory of God are humans fully alive." Human happiness, as Aristotle defined it, is the ability to use all our potentialities at a certain degree of excellence.

Step three reads: "Therefore we made the decision to turn our wills and our lives over to the care of God as we understand God."

The dynamic of these three steps is expressed in three verbs: recognize, believe, and decide: to recognize our powerlessness, to believe in a higher power, to decide to turn our life over to that higher power.

Developing Trust

The twelve-step program, especially the first three steps, is a program to implement hope for those who find life hopeless, to implement trust for those who have found that there is nothing in which they can trust, least of all themselves. It is a very pragmatic program aimed at helping people to reexperience hope and trust. It is important to note the relation between hope and trust. Hope is a sort of generic virtue by which I believe that my life has direction, purpose, and meaning. As Vaclav Havel put it: "Hope is an orientation of the spirit, an orientation of the heart. It is not the conviction that something will turn out well, but the certainty that something makes sense regardless of how it turns out."[6] The opposite of hope is despair (without hope). I hope that there is ultimate meaning in life and in death and I can depend on it.

The virtue of trust takes us a step beyond hope. Trust has to do with trusting in someone. Trust brings in the personal dimension. *I trust that someone is reliable; they will be there for me; they won't let me down; I can depend on them.*

As gay people, our ability to practice twelve-step spirituality is above all else involved with the virtue of trust. In his book *Does God Exist?* Hans Kung makes the point that the essential human psychological foundation and presupposition for faith is trust.[7] Erik Erikson, dealing with developmental psychology, claims that the first task of the human infant is to learn basic trust, the cornerstone of a psychologically healthy personality. Without it, a decent human life is impossible. No deep intimacy, no true friendship, no vital faith is possible unless we take the risk of trusting.

A fundamental trust that life is good comes to us as a gift. Infants learn to trust life insofar as they are truly loved and cared for by their parents. But maintaining a sense of fundamental trust in the universe is a lifelong task. None of us grow up without some wounding of our ability to trust. We all must struggle to achieve and maintain our ability to trust. Despite uncertainty, pain, sorrow, sickness, and death, we must trust that life is good and that love can triumph even over the grave. Our last action in life should be an act of loving trust. In the words of the *Te Deum*: *"In te Domine speravi, non confundar ab aeternum"* ("In you, Lord, I have hoped, I shall never be let down in all eternity").

Trust is the most difficult virtue for me personally. My fundamental trust in the universe was shattered by my mother's death when I was four years old. I have been working all my life on the spiritual task of reestablishing hope and trust. I remember when I was in group therapy, we had one exercise in which you were to close your eyes and fall over backward and "trust" that the other members of the group would catch you. I never did it; I still cannot do it.

Gay men and lesbians face a unique challenge to their ability to trust creation. Since we do not choose our sexual orientation, we experience it as a given, a part of our created reality, in fact, the most important part, since it influences our ability to give and receive love and to experience intimacy. As we grow up in a homophobic culture and a homophobic church, we are told that there is something wrong with the way we were created, that our very being, as a recent Vatican document phrased it, is "an orientation to evil."

Insofar as our culture leads us to experience our sexual orientation as negative, and we see ourselves as sinful, sick, or evil, we will necessarily experience a deep crisis in our ability to trust the creator. Consequently, if gay men or lesbian women take this church teaching seriously and identify with it, they must see themselves as created by God with an "orientation to evil." This would make God totally unworthy of trust. Scripture says, if anyone loves they know God, because God is love. But *we* are told: If you gay men and lesbian women follow your natural inclination to love, you will know evil and be eternally separated from God. A God who would create us with an intrinsic orientation to evil would be a sadistic God, a God who inspires fear, mistrust, and hatred, a God totally unworthy of our hope and trust, not a loving God.

If we accept this teaching of the Church, then we have a right to harbor a basic distrust in life. And we will be tempted to develop an attitude of cynicism, self-hate, and mutual cruelty. On top of this, the AIDS crisis will further threaten to destroy our hope and trust in a God of love and enslave us once again to a god of fear.

For some, AIDS has become a symbol of what they feel to be an intrinsic disorder in gay men's affectionate and loving feelings for each other. A paranoid spirit of mutual distrust can enter deeply into our lives, further endangering any possibility of achieving true intimacy with each other. Like hope, the opposite of trust is despair: despair in life, despair in love, despair of any true happiness, and ultimately despair in God Him/Herself.

The only alternative for gay people is to go the other route and refuse to despair. Listen carefully to these words of the Book of Wisdom:

> *Yes, you love all that exists,*
> *and nothing that you have made disgusts you,*
> *since if you had hated something, you would not*
> *have made it.*
> *And how could a thing subsist, had you not*
> *willed it?*
> *Or how be preserved, if not called forth by you?*
> *No, you spare all, since all is yours, Lord, lover*
> *of life!*
> *For your imperishable spirit is in everything!*
> *(11:24–12:1)*

Despite all the temptations to despair, we must choose to trust that life is good and our gayness is a gift and not a curse. We must refuse to believe that the God whose love we experience daily can be sadistic. Because of our gayness, if we so choose, we can achieve an even greater trust of self, body, nature, the cosmos, and God. We can even learn to trust that our death, when it comes, is in the natural order of things and will "work unto good," leading us to a new life as Jesus promised: "Father / I want those you have given me / to be with me where I am" (John 17:24).

As Matthew Fox observed: "Who knows more about the beauty of creation and New Creation than those who have been told verbally and nonverbally by religion and society that the way they were created was a mistake and even sinful?"[8] The struggle is first of all one to achieve self-trust, a struggle to hear and believe what God is saying to us directly every day through our experience of life. Our greatest enemy is our own interiorized homophobia and self-hatred. As Henri Nouwen put it: "Self-rejection is the greatest enemy of the spiritual life because it contradicts the sacred voice that calls us the 'Beloved.' Being the Beloved expresses the core truth of our existence."[9]

The primary teacher in the Church is not the hierarchy; it is the Holy Spirit, and the Spirit dwells in our hearts and speaks to us through our own experience. Our struggle with trust is a struggle to recognize ourselves as gay persons with divine dignity and responsibility, to see our gayness itself as a blessing and not as a curse, a blessing for which we should be grateful to God. We must learn as gay persons to celebrate our existence.

So the challenge to us is to learn to trust and hope despite all the negative messages we receive. We cannot get our hope and trust from any message that comes to us from outside; on the contrary most of the messages we receive from family, church, and culture are contaminated with homophobia. Even the translations of sacred Scripture have been contaminated by homophobia. If we listen to these voices and believe in them, we destroy ourselves.

Therefore, we must, to use a phrase of St. Bernard of Clairveau, "learn to drink from our own wells." We must learn to place our trust in our own direct experience of life and what those experiences reveal to us. We must trust that the higher power speaks to us immediately and directly through our own experience and that these experiences are the only unpolluted water we can drink from. In the process of drinking from the well of our own experiences we must try to relearn step by step to trust God and hear what God is saying to us directly. As described earlier, this is using what an ancient Christian doctrine called "discernment of spirits."

The way to know God and to become intimate with God is to listen carefully to what your own emotions are telling you. God speaks to us primarily not through our intellect but through our hearts, and it is by listening with our hearts that we can hear what God is saying. If our experience brings with it feelings of deep joy and peace and quiet, then we know that the message coming through our heart is God saying, "Right on!" You are one with the Spirit of God and there is real intimacy.

However, if you perform an action that contradicts the Spirit of God at the very heart of your being, then you will know turmoil, depression, and sadness. If you have stayed with me to this point in the book, you must have already made that commitment. You have chosen to grow in intimacy with God, to achieve the greatest possible intimacy with God. You can now trust God and trust that your own heart will lead you in this enterprise. But you must learn how to listen to your heart and trust what your own heart is telling you, believe it, and go with it.

There is a shadow side to the virtues of trust and hope. Trusting is risky. Kirkegaard compares an act of faith with a "leap in the dark." It is difficult to trust God, when there is so much evil in the world. However, God has promised us that no matter how much evil is in our lives, individually and collectively, the outcome will always be a greater good than evil. This is my trust: that ultimate good will vanquish evil. I want to trust and to hope. I cry out to God: I hunger and thirst for the gift of trust and hope! This is not a yearning that we have to look for in a special way. This yearning is open to everyone. This yearning is at the very heart of our being.

Consecrate Your Longing

As Gerald May says in his book *Addiction and Grace*, the only thing we can bring to this journey toward intimacy with God that is within our own human power is our desire, our longing. It is very important for us to get in touch with our yearning. To use an expression May uses: "We must consecrate our yearning!"[10] We must get in touch with the fact that the deepest yearning of the heart of every human being is a yearning for intimacy with the divine and nothing else but God Him/Herself can fulfill that yearning.

All addiction is a form of idolatry. It is an attempt to get your needs met through objects that are incapable of fulfilling them. It is very important to detach your yearning from its addictive object and point it directly toward the divine, to yearn for union with the divine and love that yearning.

Maurice Blondel always emphasized that between the categories of being and nonbeing there is a third category of being called privation.[11] Privation is a paradoxical "absence in presence" or conversely "presence in absence." Privation can be defined as "the absence of that which ought to be." If we are deprived of something, we long for it and we can define what it is we long for. Like a missing piece of a jigsaw puzzle, if we see it we immediately recognize it. Privation is like a hole inside us that needs to be filled up.

Privation is the direct and immediate source of our knowledge of God. Our knowledge of God is based on what we are deprived of, what we need and don't have, what we are yearning for, what we have a hunger and thirst for and have not yet achieved. Our real knowledge of God has little to do with any intellectual definition. All the great mystics saw our efforts to capture God with our thoughts and concepts as self-defeating. They recommended that in prayer we should empty our minds of all thoughts and concepts and enter the "cloud of unknowing." Our real knowledge of God comes from the hunger and thirst within ourselves. In the words of Psalm 63:

> *God, you are my God, I pine for you;*
> *my heart thirsts for you,*
> *my body longs for you,*
> *as a land parched, dreary and waterless.*

Our real spiritual life consists of being in touch with that hunger and thirst, not letting anything fill it in or block it off, or hide it from us. Rather we must strive to be in touch with that hunger and thirst, to consecrate it by converting it intentionally into prayer and identifying with it. Feel the deprivation and turn it into prayer. Turn it into a request: "Amen; come, Lord Jesus" (Rev. 22:20). The Bible tells us: "Ask, and it will be given to you; search, and you will find; knock, and the door will be open to you" (Luke 11:9). To get the full import of a biblical statement, it is always helpful to consider its negative. If you don't ask, you will not receive. If you don't knock, it will not be open to you. God waits on our freedom. We must take the initiative of inviting God in.

One of the most important tasks of our spiritual life is to get in touch with that hunger and thirst for the divine. In the words of St. Augustine, "You made us for yourself, O Lord, and our hearts will never rest, until they rest in you." We must enter into that desire and affirm it, so that it becomes one with what we are out of our freedom.

Recently during the Easter vigil (the liturgy at sundown on the Saturday before Easter Sunday) I heard this passage from the Psalms: "Like the deer panteth after the living waters, my heart thirsts for you, O my Lord" (Ps. 41:2). Suddenly, I was in touch with a profound longing for union with God; a longing that was at the same time painful and pleasurable, and I began to cry. I am grateful to God for that moment and see it as a great grace. Since that time, I am consciously aware that what I want is intimacy with God and I will not settle for anything less. I am aware that being in touch with that longing is already a kind of awareness of God through privation. That awareness is already God's gift and promise. All other touches of intimacy in my life, intimacies of family, friendships, and human lovers are foretastes of that ultimate intimacy. But the only intimacy that can completely fill my heart is the intimacy with God.

In my experience as a psychotherapist, I am aware that one of the most frequent causes of the breakdown of a human relationship is that we are asking our limited human lover to be God for us and meet all our needs. The most that we can expect from each other is that we will accompany each other on our journey through life and be a foretaste for each other of what intimacy with God is all about.

The theologian Paul Tillich, writing about hope, says that the best part of our spiritual life is waiting with our longing, just waiting patiently.[12] Our best prayer is not the prayer where we ask for something or use words. Our best prayer is where we are deeply in touch with the longing inside ourselves and wait there. "Be still, attend the Lord, and wait patiently for him" (Ps. 37:7). This is the heart of the spiritual life, its special dynamic. Waiting demands patience and patience demands stillness within ourselves. Tillich claims there are two kinds of waiting, a passive waiting in laziness and a receiving waiting in openness, an expecting.

The whole spirit of the advent season is an expectant waiting for the coming of the Lord. Even so, I am not always certain I am ready yet. I still experience fear that needs to be worked through and overcome with God's grace. If I am still dealing with a God of fear, it is because I have not yet freed myself from superego shame and guilt. My interiorized self-hatred and homophobia prevent me from loving myself. So I project out unto God that He/She will also find me unlovable and reject me.

Those who wait passively in laziness prevent the coming of what they are waiting for. By waiting in quiet tension, open to every encounter, we are doing all in our power to bring about the coming of that which we wait for. Such waiting in openness and hope does what no willpower can do for our own development. This is how we grow, mature, deepen our spiritual development.

Spiritual life then is very simple. We should spend a lot of time just being in touch with our longing, be open to it and waiting. Ask God to come and meet that deep deprivation within us. We are like a desert waiting for the rain to come and soak in. We are a hunger waiting to be filled. The more seriously the great religious men of the past took their own transformation, using their will power to achieve it, the more they failed and fell into hopelessness and despair.

The Role of God and Gratitude

One frequently heard criticism of twelve-step spirituality programs is that they are too spiritual, that people should not be encouraged to depend on anything but themselves: *"We don't need anybody or anything else. We especially don't need a higher power. We can go it alone!"* they say. I have news for them! A.A. and other twelve-step programs are only successful because they recognize that we are powerless by ourselves. Only when we open ourselves up to God and invite God in will we discover that things happen which could never happen before.

What gives us the right to such hope for inner renewal after all our failures? Again, there is only one answer: God's mercy and goodness. Trust in God's promise; wait in inner stillness with poised tension and openness toward what we can only receive as a gift.

When renewal comes, our only response should be gratitude. We cannot make the mistake of pride, the belief that we receive God's gifts because of our own efforts and specialness. Our pride ties God's hands and can prevent the giving of the gift. If, however, we recognize that what comes to us is a gift based on God's goodness and mercy and not on our merits, then we will experience gratitude, not pride. "The Almighty has done great things for me," Mary says in the Magnificat, and we also, once we have recovered from our addiction or attachment, can say God has done great things for us. *I am a recovering alcoholic; I am recovering from my addictions, thanks be to God.*

When I was last in Ireland visiting my relatives, everybody went about constantly repeating that phrase, "Thanks be to God!" I thought to myself. It is probably just a pious tradition with no real meaning for those who are saying it. Then I found out that one of my relative's neighbors had fallen from his hayloft and broken his back. His sons had carried him five years in a row to the shrine of Our Lady of Knock for a cure, and five years in a row they had carried him back. But on the sixth year he walked back, cured.

A lady bicycled out to the countryside from Boyle and stopped by my cousin's farm and asked: "Where can I see the man who was miraculously cured by Our Lady?" "He's out mowing the hay in the next field," my cousin told the lady. After the woman left, my cousin fell to the ground in laughter. "What are you laughing at?" I asked. "You can't see a miracle," he said. "He went to Knock; he asked Our Lady for a cure; he persisted, so Our Lady cured him and now he is out in the field mowing the hay for his family and ten children." It dawned on me then and there that these people had such deep faith and trust that they took a miraculous intervention of the higher power for granted. There was no chance of swollen egos or feeling better than others. There was just gratitude. If you persist and are patient in your prayers, they will be answered.

I'm now aware that one of the special gifts that has come out of all the suffering surrounding the AIDS epidemic is the awareness that to be healed is not necessarily to be cured. There is something else going on. Earlier I quoted Vaclav Havel in his address to the U.S. Congress as saying: "Hope is an orientation of the spirit; an orientation of the heart. It is not the conviction that something will turn out well, but the certainty that something makes sense regardless of how it turns out."[13]

Our faith and trust in God must be such that we are certain that God hears our prayers and responds to them in some way, even if that response is not visible to us. As John Carmody put it in his article "A Theology of Illness":

> . . . neither ill nor well can we know how God is working things out. . . . And this essential, unavoidable ignorance turns out, like all God's other ways with us, to be a blessing. We have to let God be God. . . . There is a time to speak, but also a time to hold silence—to take it to your bosom like a love. There is a time to assault God, accuse God, but also a time to wait and leave God free. Ask the Spirit of God to teach you God's times. At least try to want to leave God free.[14]

A life devoted to waiting for God will not always be joyful or easy. We will struggle between moments of hope and moments of doubt and despair. But that struggle is a symptom that the new has already taken hold in us. A spiritual growth is going on, a deepening of the union of what God is and what I am.

In *Addiction and Grace*, May stresses that the critical point in the twelve-step process is the moment when you give up your addiction, when you get from the higher power the strength and courage not to touch the drink or drug or to come out of the closet. The moment you free yourself from an addiction, you liberate the attachment power in your psyche and you will experience a deep and painful longing.[15] The Bible speaks of the man who had a devil cast out, but immediately twelve other devils came and took its place. In other words as soon as you free yourself from an addiction, there will be an immediate temptation to reattach quickly. Eric Fromm speaks of "flight from freedom."[16] We are frightened by freedom. We are frightened by the openness, the insecurity; we are frightened by the longing and the spaciousness. Consequently, we are tempted to reattach immediately. The moment of freedom is also a moment of great temptation.

May's key message is that the moment you free yourself from an addiction, it is very important spiritually speaking to *consecrate* your openness and your freedom. Name that to which you want to become attached and do so out of your freedom and conscious choice. Name your ultimate love object as God Him/Herself.

There is a need to consecrate your drive, your longing, and to be able to abide in it, to feel the hunger and the thirst, feel the loneliness, the alienation, the privation. Do not go out immediately and find another substance or person to become addicted to. Tell yourself: My heart will never rest until it rests in you, O my God! Remember the great commandment: You shall love the Lord, your God, with all your heart, soul, and mind.

Our constant temptation is to try to substitute something else for God, something we have more control over, in order to gain meaning and security in this world. The process of consecrating my desire is merely a matter of identifying the fact that what I ultimately want, both in this life and for all eternity, is union with God and that nothing else can fulfill me. It does not mean that I cannot want anything else. I yearn for a beef steak, a drink, a human lover. But underneath all these human needs there is the longing for union with God. It does mean that I cannot know fulfillment until I achieve that union with God.

This is what is meant by the biblical command to "choose life!"[17] Every morning when you wake up, put yourself in the presence of God and say: "I love you and I will not settle for anything or anyone less than you!" Frequently during the day call to mind the presence of God, your lover, and make a return act of love. And going to bed at night thank God, your lover, for all the gifts and graces of that day, especially for the gift of God's love. Of course, to live out this life of conscious consecration to a God of love presupposes that we are liberated from the god of fear. Perfect love casts out all fear, true, but it is equally true that perfect fear casts out all love.

The Philosophical Dialectic of Freedom

In our search for self-fulfillment, according to Maurice Blondel, we come across a category of human choices and actions that are simultaneously "necessary and impossible," necessary if we are to achieve human fulfillment but impossible to achieve by human means alone.[18] This is a difficult category of action to hold onto. We are tempted to insist that if these choices are necessary for human fulfillment, then they must be capable of being achieved by human means alone. If, on the other hand, they are impossible to achieve by human means alone, then they cannot be necessary. Despite this internal contradiction this category of action spontaneously arises within human consciousness in our striving to achieve our destiny. The only way to move forward when we encounter that category is to open ourselves to a paradoxically transcendent/immanent source of energy and power.

The key member of this category of action is the action of love. Genuine human love is essential to human fulfillment but impossible by human means alone. This is why Scripture can say,

> My dear friends,
> let us love one another,
> since love is from God
> and everyone who loves
> is a child of God and knows God.
> Whoever fails to love does not know God,
> because God is love. (1 John 4:7–8)

Within the immanent context of the dialectic of human action, the source of the necessary ideal of God as transcendent power is understood as our projecting out of all the unused and unusable potentialities of the human spirit. "Humans can never succeed by their own powers alone to place in their willed action all that which is at the origin of their voluntary activity."[19] Thus, God represents that which is necessary for the human, if we are to achieve a state of self-adequation, and at the same time that which humans find impossible to achieve by their own powers alone. By self-adequation Blondel understood that we achieve a harmony between what we have willed and the deepest longings in our psyche. "What we know of God is the surplus of interior life which demands its employment; we cannot, then, know God without willing in some way to become one with God."[20]

This insight brings out the extraordinary wisdom in twelve-step spirituality. Having discovered our own powerlessness over addiction we reach out for the help of a "higher power." In Blondelian terms this could be defined as reaching within for a "lower depth" in our own psyche where the divine power which transcends our finite ego dwells within us. Further, Blondel would hold that the need to do so not only applies to overcoming addiction but is essential to every human's effort to reach out in genuine love in the process of achieving our destiny. "Our God," Blondel wrote, "lies within us and the only way to become one with our God, is to become one with our authentic self."

> To equal ourselves and to be saved we humans must go beyond ourselves. To consent to the invasion of all that stands for a life that is prior and a will that is superior to our own, is our way of contributing to our own creation. To will all that we will in complete sincerity of heart is to place in us the being and the action of God. No doubt it does cost something, since we do not perceive how profoundly this will is our own. But one must give all for the all. Life has a divine value, and despite the weakness of pride and sensuality, humanity is generous enough to want to belong more completely to the one who exacts more of it.[21]

CHAPTER 11

OPENING *a* DIALOGUE

between the FEMINIST *and the*

MASCULINE UNDERSTANDINGS

of TWELVE-STEP SPIRITUALITY

In the Epilogue, we will deal at some length with the fact that the last three thousand years of Western culture have been under the control of the masculine archetype with a corresponding repression of the feminine. We have reached the end of that historical process and the unfolding of the feminine archetype has begun. This new unfolding of the feminine is taking place in every aspect of our culture, but especially in our spirituality. It should come as no surprise that within the twelve-step spiritual movement there is a feminist challenge to the traditional formulation of twelve-step spirituality. For the most part the women and men who are making this challenge are people who have used twelve-step programs and have found them critical to their survival and liberation. Their aim then, is not to discredit the twelve steps. On the contrary, their aim is to open up ways of thinking about recovery that could be especially helpful to women.

Men can experience that challenge, like any challenge to change, as somewhat fearful and anxiety provoking. But, I believe, if we have the courage to listen and the willingness to grow and develop, we will find that challenge an extraordinary opportunity to mature to the fullness of our humanity.

We are in a special moment of spiritual liberation in terms of women's liberation. This, like gay liberation, is, I believe, the work of the Holy Spirit in our day. All of us are being challenged to come into contact with the feminine not just outside ourselves but also within ourselves. This is the primary process I am involved with in the case of many of the gay male clients who come to me for therapy. At the heart of most cases of internalized male homophobia lies an even deeper and more intense repressed "feminaphobia." Many of my male clients have thoroughly repressed the feminine and are afraid of it.

Many of my gay male clients in their earliest years were very open to and in touch with the feminine self. However, because of the homophobia of their family, church, and culture they had to learn to try to control and repress any evidence of that feminine self. This meant trying to suppress all feelings, all creativity, and all spirituality, and also trying to live in their heads by developing their intellectual skills and compulsively staying out of touch with all feelings. The only way to health and fullness of life for these clients is to unrepress and live out that previously dreaded feminine dimension of themselves. I believe that the dialogue going on at present within A.A. between feminist and traditional understandings of twelve-step spirituality gives us a unique opportunity to understand the principal challenges that feminists are bringing to help us all grow to complete maturity.

The Feminist Critique of the Twelve Steps

In her article "Twelve Steps for Women Alcoholics," Gail Unterberger claims that research on women addicts found that many of them find the A.A. and other twelve-step groups to be overly masculine in both their approach and their form of spirituality.[1] The latest research on women with addictions shows that these women's concerns and needs frequently differ substantially from those of male addicts.

According to Unterberger, what women find especially attractive about A.A. is its democratic spirit and its lack of any hierarchy. Everyone present in the room is a total equal to all others. This is best expressed in the second of the twelve traditions (the twelve traditions were a later effort to give explicit formulations to the principles of A.A.): "For our group purpose there is but one ultimate authority—a loving God as may be expressed in our group conscience. Our leaders are but trusted servants, they do not govern."[2] This tradition is kept by rotating all leadership functions within the group.

Unterberger believes that women also find attractive the placing of the common welfare first. *"Our common welfare should come first: personal recovery depends upon A.A. unity."*[3] The role of "anonymity," that the personal identity of anyone in the group should not be made known to anyone outside the group, as a means to avoid anyone using A.A. for ego trips, is another attractive feature.[4] As stated in tradition twelve, "Anonymity is the spiritual foundation of all our traditions, ever reminding us to place principles above personalities."[5]

However, Unterberger observes that women alcoholics are more likely to suffer from low self-esteem than their male counterparts. Depression and self-derogation may lead to feeling a lack of purpose in life, and thus to substance abuse. Female alcoholics tend to turn their anger on themselves rather than on others, with resulting anxiety and guilt. They frequently feel inadequate to the point of futility. "Our male-dominated society confers upon women a status subordinated to men: women of color or of differing sexual orientation suffer even greater oppression. Therefore, addicted women need a spirituality that empowers them, lifts their self-esteem and gives them a sense of identity and worth."[6]

In her book, *She Who Is: The Mystery of God in Feminist Theological Discourse*, the feminist theologian Elizabeth Johnson points out that the spiritual concept of "conversion" for women takes on a radically different meaning from its classical use in spirituality, where it typically denoted the process of divesting oneself of ego in order to be open to divine grace.[7] This meaning is useful when dealing with the temptation to pride and self-assertion against others. The prideful person feels no need for God's help.

If pride is the primary block to God, as it frequently is in the heterosexual male self-image, then indeed decentering the rapacious self and recognizing our dependence on God is the work of grace. But Johnson observes that "the situation is quite different when this language is applied to persons already relegated to the margins of significance and excluded from the exercise of self-definition. For such persons, the language of conversion as loss of self, turning from self-love, functions in an ideological way to rob them of power, maintaining them in a subordinate position to the benefit of those who rule."[8]

Joseph Campbell in his book *The Hero's Journey* tells the story of men who are brought low in order to realize salvation. For heterosexual men, admitting powerlessness indicates their readiness for God to move in and save them. But women, says Campbell, must take the opposite journey. "They need to stand up, affirm their will and empower themselves."[9]

Consequently, many women find the original wording of the first of the twelve steps: "We admit that we are powerless over alcohol—that our lives have become unmanageable," can be counterproductive for women. For the traditional phrase of introduction: "I am John and I am an alcoholic!" some women would prefer an introduction along the lines of: "I am Jane; I am a person with an alcoholic problem." Whereas the traditional statement identifies the whole of one's self with the problem, the revised statement separates off a positive self-image from the alcoholic problem. For this reason, Jean Kirkpatrick, founder of "Women for Sobriety," designed "thirteen steps" with the conscious purpose of helping women to enhance their self-esteem: "We have a drinking problem that once had us."[10]

Perhaps the most important criticism that feminists make of the original twelve-step program is that its theology is implicitly patriarchal. Gail Unterberger finds that A.A.'s twelve steps insinuate a hierarchical, domination-submission model of the individual's relationship to God. In traditional groups God is always referred to as male, and God's activities are described in stereotypically masculine terms. Furthermore, the spirituality described in the steps can be seen as exclusively individualistic. A.A. portrays the individual in a one-to-one relationship with God, before whom the individual person must admit total powerlessness. The alcoholic then comes to "believe in" (cognitively) a God who is omnipotent and has the ability to "restore sanity" to the addict, a God to whom one must surrender one's will. As some understand it, the program then calls for the individual to admit guilt and wrongdoings and humbly plead to be imbued with God's power. Through vigilance, prayer, and meditation, one continues the process of recovery. This process requires explicit relationships with other group members only for steps five and twelve. *Step Five*: "Admitted to God, to ourselves, and to another human being the exact nature of our wrongs." *Step Twelve*: "Having had a spiritual awakening as a result of these steps, we try to carry this message to other alcoholics, and to practice these principles in all our affairs."[11]

God is portrayed here as the transcendent judge and power broker. Recovery then, hinges on how well the individual submits to God. The addict him- or herself is portrayed as "a lone ranger on a personal spiritual journey," albeit a journey paralleling the journey of others. Adult women can find the image of a paternalistic and domineering God harmful; it hinders the development of the mature sense of self that addicted women lack. The call for submission can all too easily blend in with other unhealthy demands to submit that are destructive to women's self-image.

The Communal Dimension

Feminist revisions of the twelve steps stress the communal, not the individual, nature of the process of recovery. The communal aspect, implicit in the "we" of the first three steps and touched on in the first tradition, is made explicit and central. Members are dependent on each other in the twelve-step process, and women claim that this mutuality is, in fact, more essential to the A.A. recovery process than the addict's independent spirituality.

As Gail Unterberger observes, feminist psychology and spirituality focus on how God acts through our relationships with others in community. Because women's sense of self relies on relationships, a solitary journey model of recovery is inadequate; it denies the essential role of the healing community. For the second traditional step: "We came to believe that a power greater than ourselves could restore us to sanity," Unterberger proposes substituting the feminist revision: "We realize we needed to turn to others for help."[12]

For women, to look above for power has almost always meant to look to men. Women need to develop faith in themselves and in their relationships with other women. Women are involved in a long journey of learning to trust. "Women have been socialized to discredit the value of other women's care and support, preferring to depend on men for affirmation of self-worth. To learn to trust themselves and other women, women repeatedly need to receive sincere affirmation from other women, survive open conflict and initiate gentle confrontation."[13]

The gay community has had similar experiences. Gay men, like women, have frequently been socialized to discredit each other's care and support and to depend on straight men for affirmation of self-worth. To learn to trust themselves and other gay men, gay men need a frequent experience of gay affirmation and support within the context of a loving community.

A feminist revision of the twelve steps makes paramount an idea that is implicit in traditional A.A. twelve steps but never was made explicit: the members are dependent upon one another, upon community. Although the first three steps that we dealt with never mentioned community, the concept is implicit in the word *we*. *We* are powerless; *we* have faith in a higher power; *we* ask that higher power to come and empower us. That *we* is all the people here together in the room. In her book *Witness to the Fire*, about her recovery from alcoholism, Linda Schierse Leonard begins by saying:

> *I turned and asked help from others whom I knew had sunk to similar depths, yet who were recovering. Up until then I was so angry at God for having "let me down" that I was in rebellion. I could not open myself to any higher power at all. But with other recovering addicts I felt the miracle that happens when people come together to share the stories of their suffering, their descent toward death, and their return to life. In those meetings I felt the higher power of love. These stories inspired me and opened my heart with hope.*[14]

Leonard could not turn to God initially, because God for her was a masculine, patriarchal, fearful symbol. Many gay men have a similar experience with the transcendent god of fear. We, too, find the effectiveness of A.A. in the nonjudgmental community of compassion. We first turn to our brothers and sisters. We begin to have trust in an immanent God of love because of our experience of human love and compassion within the A.A. community.

Women want to make explicit that there is a first step, that of turning to each other, and then finding God in each other, instead of going directly to God. The attitude that *"I don't fool around with any subordinates in this organization! I go directly to the top,"* is very male. Women turn to each other and form a sisterhood and then get empowered by the Spirit. The Spirit, with their free cooperation, moves out of them toward their sisters, and it is in the mutual love and compassion that they have for each other that they find God. They find a God that they can live with that does not make them feel inferior. "For where two or three meet in my name, I am there among them" (Matt. 18:20).

The Image of God

Central to all the revisions that feminist critics suggest is the image of God. Gail Unterberger suggests that a more appropriate image of God for addicted women would be the Holy Spirit, who ignites the spark of hope within each woman and breathes life through the group, working for each member's well-being and recovery. Through the experience of self-in-relation, participants find liberation and the healing power of a community empowered by the Spirit; and the Spirit is the only member of the Trinity that traditionally has not been symbolized as male.

The most important revision, then, in the feminist understanding of the twelve steps is a transition from a predominantly transcendent image of God to a predominantly immanent image. Blondel's insight into the radical nature of human freedom led him to accept what he called "the principle of immanence" as the fundamental methodological principle governing his philosophy of free action. He formulated that principle in these words:

> *Nothing can impose itself on a human; nothing can demand the assent of our intellect or the consent of our will which does not find its source from within ourselves.*
>
> *That necessity which appears to me as a tyrannous constraint, that obligation which at first appears despotic, in the last analysis, it is necessary that I un-*

*derstand it as manifesting and activating the most
profound reality of my own will; otherwise it will be
my destruction.*[15]

Anything that presents itself from without as essential to the
achievement of human destiny and happiness must correspond to a need
in the dynamic of the human will or, on the psychological level, to a
profoundly felt desire at the depth of the human psyche. Blondel did
not hesitate to apply this methodological principle of immanence to any
manifestation of the divine will. Although the divine will must manifest
itself as in some way distinct from and transcendent to our finite will,
yet that revelation, if it is not to destroy our freedom and integrity, must
be made in some way from within our consciousness of self and prove
capable of being assimilated into our free self-positing. A perfect example of the violation of the principle of immanence occurs when
Church authorities, claiming to speak with God's authority, make the
claim that gays and lesbians must totally suppress and deny their gayness
in order to achieve salvation. Whereas, what the Spirit of God is saying
to gays and lesbians from within their experience is that they must accept
and live out their orientation in order to achieve their destiny.

The concept of God as Spirit immanent in our psyche, yet
transcending our finite ego from within, leads to the concept of God as
the "lower depths" of our psyche rather than an external "higher power."
A central message of the New Testament was that this Spirit of God can
only be found when we reach out in compassion and love to our fellow
human beings: "In truth I tell you, in so far as you did this to one of the
least of these my brothers and sisters, you did it to me" (Matt: 25:40).
Consequently, this Spirit's power can be experienced best in a communal
setting of love.

Love is at the heart of every twelve-step meeting; we reach
out, we are there for each other, we are compassionate, loving, nonjudgmental. That's why I frequently believe that the most effective
church in town is not necessarily the liturgy upstairs in the sanctuary
but the A.A. meeting in the basement.

Martin Buber frequently made the point that God Him/
Herself as absolute is rarely, if ever, the direct object of our choice. But

we can encounter God by absolutely committing ourselves to finite others. Thus, God is to be found not in the *I* or the *thou*, but in the relating represented by the connecting "-", in the that-which-lies-between (the *dazwischen*) in the expression *I-Thou*.[16] Carter Heyward makes a similar point when she suggests that we best express what God means, not in the noun God, but in the verb "Godding."[17]

In his final theory of interpersonal communion, Blondel underlines the necessity of the indwelling of the Spirit of God within consciousness, if any real intersubjective communion is to be considered possible among humans. "It is impossible to enter really into contact with another human being, in fact, it is impossible to enter into contact with oneself, without passing through the *Uniquely Necessary*, who must become our unique will."[18] The refusal of the Spirit of God can only result in an isolation of the person and shut him or her in a false subjectivity and interiority which is in reality an avaricious possession of the self. The result is that modern world of solitude and hostility, a world without meeting and true presence, a world of refusal and discontinuity. "The Egoist is disconcerted by the very thought of so many hostile egos, and despite all the clarity of our knowledge, we remain enclosed in solitude and obscurity."[19]

The only way, according to Blondel, to escape this prison of self is by communication with the transcendent who is both immanent in self and a bridge to the other. "One cannot be for oneself or for another without being for God first of all."[20] We cannot communicate on the level of real existence with anyone unless it be with and by the Spirit of God.

However, it is important to note that if Blondel insists on a priority in being of a communion with the divine Spirit, he is by no means implying a priority in time, nor a psychological priority of divine love over human love. We do not have to love God first before we can experience true human love. Blondel repeatedly insisted that the divine Spirit would be present wherever there was a true act of love, with or without an explicit faith-commitment by the individual to be open to that Spirit. It is, however, necessarily implicit in the living reality of every free human action of love. It is not necessary, he tells us, to have resolved conceptually any metaphysical problem concerning the existence of God in order to live metaphysically. The true resolution of the problem of unity by love from any one of the three points of view possible, love of self, of God, or of another human, necessarily involves a vital solution of that problem from all three viewpoints.

But undoubtedly the ordinary level on which the problem and its resolution are posed psychologically is within the context of human love and human community. "Without that love which is active within the members of humanity, there is no God for humans; the one who does not love his neighbor has no life in him."[21]

In any human encounter, therefore, if a genuine interpersonal bond of human love is factually established, then it necessarily implies an implicit resolution of the option in favor of the divine Spirit. This is also the case even when there is no explicit psychological awareness of the underlying option in favor of the presence of the divine Spirit. "At the very root of being, in the common practice of life, in the secret logic of consciousness, without God there is no fellow human being for us humans."

A charitable act of self-giving, in order to be real, must incarnate itself in a material gesture. And it is this kind of act that occurs constantly at every twelve-step meeting. Any true act of compassionate love necessarily involves the same negation of the selfish ego which is in fact a positive opening up to the Spirit of love; such an act must lead to an experiential awareness of the presence of that Spirit.

As a result, this act goes well beyond an attitude of justice only in which one considers the impersonal character of the other, and his or her abstract dignity as a human being. A true act of love must contain the will to place oneself at the service of the other. This is the price one must pay in order to become in reality an instrument of the action of divine unifying love.

The Gay and Lesbian Synthesis

When I first read about the feminist critique of the twelve steps, I was struck by the fact that, although I found the traditional formulation powerful and valid, I found that the feminist revisions spoke to my needs as a gay man. When I presented Unterberger's revised twelve steps to a variety of gay men's groups, they responded enthusiastically to the way the steps directly addressed gay men's spiritual needs. Gay men and lesbian women understand and synthesize in their experience both the traditional and the feminist versions of the twelve steps.

The twelve steps were drawn up originally by a group of straight men, for the most part, in the midwest. Therefore, the way the twelve steps were formulated reflects the limited but valid view of life, sobriety, God, and spiritual process of American straight men from predominantly Protestant backgrounds. What these men explicitly stated in the twelve steps left implicit a great deal of what actually goes on at every A.A. meeting. The feminist critique brings out explicitly what was implicit in that original formulation. But I believe that we need to synthesize what is legitimate in the feminine with the masculine and then come up with what is the full human statement, or as I prefer to call it, the Gay Statement of the Twelve Steps.

I believe that, as gay people, we have deep masculine resources as well as feminine resources in our psyches, especially if we are accepting ourselves and out of the closet in a healthy way. Therefore, we are in a unique position to understand and accept both approaches. Consequently, I believe that gay people in the A.A. movement are in a key position to help this reconciliation. There is a danger that both sides may become too rigid in rejecting the legitimate insights of the other side. Men are in danger of overemphasizing the transcendence-submission model of spirituality. On the other hand, women are in danger of so emphasizing the immanence and identity of God with the human, that they could lose the transcendent nature of God's power and thus diminish the spiritual power of the steps.

The struggle then is to open up A.A. once again to the Spirit of God and incorporate the best insights that women have to offer without losing the spiritual power that is already present in A.A.

Many gay men can fully identify, for example, with the feminine experience of low self-esteem. We, too, tend to turn our anger in on ourselves. We frequently feel futility in our effort to fulfill the male role. We also need a spirituality that empowers us, lifts up our self-esteem, and gives us a sense of identity and worth. I think it is the fundamental need that all of us, especially women and gay men, bring to A.A. Consequently, I tend to see the feminist revision as not exclusively attached to gender difference. Rather, that revision has to do with any group that has been marginalized and has interiorized a low self-image.

The archetypal male role, which the traditional twelve steps formulated well, is the struggle of the promethean man to separate off from all states of symbiosis, attain his separate individuality and autonomy, courageously assert the maximum degree of his freedom, and defy any tyrannous attack on that freedom from without. This masculine need, I will argue in the Epilogue, is present in all humans, male and female, and has a necessary priority over the feminine agenda.

The archetypal female role, equally present in all humans, is the need to enter deeply into communities of love, communities based in our freedom and not on compulsive symbiosis; the need, if the community is to be a truly human community of love, to deny any superior versus inferior status, see every member as equal, and base all leadership on service. As Jesus put it, "Among the gentiles it is the kings who lord it over them, and those who have authority over them are given the title Benefactor. With you this must not happen. No; the greatest among you must behave as if he were the youngest, the leader as if he were the one who serves. For who is the greater: the one at table or the one who serves? The one at table, surely? Yet here am I among you as one who serves!" (Luke 22:25–27).

This feminine revision makes such great sense to me that I can fully agree with it. But I see it as in no way a derogation from the male viewpoint. The male viewpoint is valid. Women have to open themselves up to the male viewpoint because in the end, when you are on your deathbed, you must deal one-to-one with God. But men must also open themselves up to the female viewpoint. Women want to make full use of the human community. Before they can find a God they can deal with, they must find the human love we have for each other. I believe this is true for gay people also. We must free ourselves of the god of the straight world, the god of fear and coercion. We rediscover the God of love within the human community; we rediscover the Spirit of God present in each of our stories of struggle with addiction or coming out of the closet, and once again we find grounds for hope in a God of love. We come away with a deep sense of the presence of God, not a God you can grab hold of; all we have are each other, yet we experience God as present in the bonds that unite us.

PART 4

THE GAY LOVE OF GOD
AND GOD'S LOVE
OF GAYS

INTRODUCTION

HOMOSEXUALITY *and*

the NEW TESTAMENT

The Gay-Friendly Attitude of Jesus
and the Early Christian Community

All of us engaged in the spiritual dimension of gay and lesbian liberation constantly have had to deal with "Bible thumpers" who make the claim that the gay life-style is clearly condemned in the Bible as an "abomination" contrary to God's will. In his excellent book *Gay Theology without Apology*, Gary David Comstock makes the point that the Bible, written by men from within a patriarchal culture, is ridden with homophobia.[1] ▼ I agree totally with Comstock's argument, which I also propose in the first part of this book, that we can build a legitimate progay sexual ethic based on our experience within the gay community and the direct, unmediated revelation that God's Spirit makes to us. I agree also that, if it is true that Paul, for example, is unequivocally condemning homosexuality, then we must conclude that Paul is wrong in this judgment, just as we admit today that Paul was wrong in his acceptance of slavery. The time has come for the Christian community to move beyond Paul's understanding of homosexuality. ▼ But I disagree that we should just hand over the Bible to our enemies as many propose we do in the gay and lesbian community. I will never forget my joy and sense of liberation when I first read John Boswell's critique of the traditional passages used to condemn homosexuality.[2] I agree with Boswell that it can be established with good scholarship that nowhere in Scripture, the Old and the New Testaments, is there a clear condemnation of a loving relationship between two adult gay men or two lesbians. I do not agree that to undertake such a scholarly task amounts to "apologizing" for those biblical passages that appear to condemn homosexuality.[3] ▼ There is a clear condemnation in Scripture of certain types of homosexual actions, such as using rape (anal penetration) against enemies as a sign of hatred, scorn, contempt, and domination. When the Pharaoh of Egypt sat on his throne, he rested his feet on a footstool carved with images of all the tribes he had conquered including the Israelites. And the official wording for his conquest was: "The Pharaoh has anally penetrated his enemies." ▼ There is also a frequent condemnation of the use of sexuality in general and homosexuality in particular in religious fertility rites, for example, in such episodes as the Golden Calf (Exodus 32), the Flood (Gen. 6–9), and the destruction of Sodom (Gen. 19). It was a widespread belief among the pagans in biblical times that if one gave sexual pleasure to the pagan Gods usually through the

use of sacred prostitutes both male and female, they would reward the worshipers with fertility for themselves, their animals, and their fields. There is a continuous polemic in Genesis
and Exodus against the use of sex in the worship of God, a polemic Paul continues in his attack on idol worshipers in Romans
(1:18–32). The clear message of the Bible is that human
sexuality is in human hands to be used for human purposes.[4] ▼ But what Comstock seems to overlook is the possibility that despite the patriarchal and homophobic culture
that Jesus was a part of, he and his disciples did not share that
prejudice. To be sure, this possiblity is easy to overlook,
because centuries of homophobic redactors and translators
have sought to eliminate all traces of this positive attitude. A
good example of that is the history of how the sin of Sodom,
which even Jesus himself clearly understood as a sin of inhos-
pitality to the stranger (Luke 10:10–12), has been reinter-
preted for political reasons as the sin of homosexuality. I have
dealt with these negative biblical passages at length in my
book *The Church and the Homosexual.*[5] ▼ We gays need to
approach Scripture with what the feminists call "a hermeneutic
of suspicion." Our "suspicion" is that, if there was a gay-
positive attitude on the part of Jesus and his followers, every
effort would be made to bury the evidence. But, despite those
efforts, certain gay-positive elements remain in the New Testament. The first element is the fact that nowhere in the four
gospels did Jesus ever say one word of condemnation concerning homosexuality. This silence would be truly surprising,
if Jesus considered all homosexual relations as seriously sinful. He makes very strong statements of condemnation for
other human actions that he sees as necessarily contrary to
the will of his Father in heaven.

The Beloved Disciple

There are, I believe, three traces of a gay-positive attitude on Jesus' part found in the New Testament. The first is the title that John the Evangelist gives himself: "the disciple whom Jesus loved." "Peter turned and saw the disciple whom Jesus loved following them—the one who had leant back close to his chest at the supper and had said to him, 'Lord, who is it that will betray you?'" (John 21:20–21). Notice what John writes. He does not call himself the disciple who loved Jesus; rather, he claims that there was a distinct quality of love that Jesus had for him that distinguished him from all the other disciples. And the other disciples did not dispute his claim. ▼ John was the one who had the position of honor at Jesus' right at the last supper, and leaned his head on Jesus' chest. John was the one who stood at the foot of the cross with the women, when all the other men fled. And it was to John's care that Jesus committed his mother: "Seeing his mother and the disciple whom he loved standing near her, Jesus said to his mother, 'Woman, this is your son.' Then to the disciple he said, 'This is your mother.' And from that hour the disciple took her into his home" (John 19:26–27). Again it is John who is the first after the women to see the empty tomb and realize that Jesus had risen from the dead. Any one of you that has a gay sensibility will be keenly aware of the special nature of the relationship of love that united Jesus and John.

The Gay Centurion and His "Beloved Boy"

No passages in Scripture are clearer concerning the gay-positive attitude of Jesus than the two accounts of Jesus' healing of the Roman centurion's servant as recounted in Matthew (8:5–13) and in Luke (7:1–10).[6]

When he had come to the end of all he wanted the people to hear, he went into Capernaum. A centurion there had a servant, a favourite of his, who was sick and near death. Having heard about Jesus he sent some Jewish elders to him to ask him to come and heal his servant. When they came to Jesus they pleaded earnestly with him saying, "He deserves this of you, because he is well disposed towards our people; he built us our synagogue himself." So Jesus went with them, and was not very far from the house when the centurion sent word to him by some friends to say to him, "Sir, do not put yourself to any trouble because I am not worthy to have you under my roof; and that is why I did not presume to come to you myself; let my boy be cured by your giving the word. For I am under authority myself, and have soldiers under me; and I say to one man, 'Go,' and he goes; to another, 'Come here,' and he comes; to my servant, 'Do this,' and he does it." When Jesus heard these words he was astonished at him and, turning round, said to the crowd following him, "I tell you, not even in Israel have I found faith as great

as this." And when the messengers got
back to the house they found the servant
in perfect health. (Luke 7:1–10)

The words used in the Greek original of these texts
for the centurion's servant are *entimos* and *pais*. These words
could be translated as "my beloved boy" and would have
clearly indicated to Jesus that he was dealing with two men in
a homosexual relationship. Jesus expresses astonishment at
the faith of the centurion and, obviously moved by his love for
his "boy," heals the young man. ▼ A Roman centurion was
not allowed to marry during his period of service.[7] Given the
all-male nature of the Roman legions, the slave would have
been the one to see to the physical comfort of the centurion
himself. Slaves were not infrequently at the beck and call of
the sexual pleasure of their master or their mistress. It was not
unusual for the relationship of a slave and his master to grow
into one of love.[8] ▼ Here we have the most direct encounter
of Jesus Christ with someone who would today be pronounced
"gay" and Christ's reaction is acceptance of the person without judgment and even eagerness to be of assistance to restore the *pais* to health, and by implication, to fully restore the
relationship of the two, making possible the renewal of any
sexual activity which they would have enjoyed together prior
to the illness. ▼ It is important to note that Jesus does not
exempt this gay relationship from the rest of what Jesus
taught with regard to moral action, but rather opens the possibility of bringing gay relationships within the compass of
healthy and holy human love.

When Jesus saw the Centurion in Matthew, he saw someone who put the one

134

he loved ahead of himself to the point of seeking the well-being of the *pais* at considerable cost to the Roman Centurion himself. After all, this proud representative of the military might of Rome has humbled himself out of love to beg a favor from an itinerant Jewish preacher. In Luke, Jesus heard of a Centurion who also put the *pais* ahead of himself, and, who practiced justice and charity in his more general relationships with the Jewish community. These are both signs of all the attributes which Jesus has just presented in the Sermon on the Mount (Luke 6:20–38) and his definition of "The True Disciple" as one who hears his word and acts on it (Luke 6:47).[9]

Anyone who has been active in AIDS ministry is aware how often this totally unselfish gay love is played out in hospitals and clinics and homes all over the country when a gay lover is loyal to his dying companion to the end. According to the Roman law of slavery the centurion was under no legal obligation to take care of a sick slave. A sick slave could be abandoned by his or her master.[10] ▼ There is a parallel to the story of the centurion's servant in the story of the centurion Cornelius' acceptance of the faith in Acts 10. One scholar proposed that Luke in Acts 10 might be subtly proposing an alternative view of homosexual relations to that commonly supposed of Paul; the question will then arise as to whether there is a connection between his presentation of the centurion Cornelius in Acts 10 and the centurion in the seventh chapter of

Luke's gospel. ▼ There is a final ironic note to the history of this passage. At every communion rite in the Roman Catholic Church the last words that a communicant says before receiving Holy Communion are: "Lord, I am not worthy to receive you, but only say the word and I shall be healed." I believe God has a divine sense of humor and moved a Church prone to homophobia to use the faith confession of a gay man every time we receive the Lord in the Eucharist. ▼ Scholars point out that when John retells the same story all indications that we are dealing with a gay love story are repressed: the centurion becomes a royal official, the sick person becomes his son, and he is reprimanded for his lack of faith (John 4:43–54). The cover-up and repression in response to the homophobia of the culture has begun and will continue to this day.

Jesus' Family of Choice

Some of the most tender human memories of Jesus described in the four gospels are those that depict him at home with his friends Martha, Mary, and Lazarus in their home in Bethany. It is obvious that these people were Jesus' family of choice.[11] "Jesus loved Martha and her sister and Lazarus" (John 11:5). The reason for that choice was also obvious; these people had an unconditional love for Jesus and had complete faith and respect for his mission. "'Yes Lord,' [Martha] said, 'I believe that you are the Christ, the Son of God, the one who was to come into this world.'" (John 11:27). ▼ Jesus evidently did not receive such faith and respect from his biological family. In fact, we are told at one point that they thought he was crazy and intended to kidnap him and bring him home by force. "He went home again, and once more such a crowd collected that they could not even have a meal. When his relatives heard of this, they set out to take charge of him; they said, 'He is out of his mind'" (Mark 3:20–21). All four gospels record Jesus as saying: "'Who is my mother? Who are my brothers?' And stretching out his hands towards his disciples he said, 'Here are my mother and my brothers. Anyone who does the will of my Father in heaven is my brother and sister and mother'" (Matt. 12:46–50). ▼ We gather from the gospels that the house of Mary, Martha, and Lazarus was Jesus' favorite resting place, and he frequently went there to relax and be among friends. But who were the members of Jesus' family of choice? The first was Mary. The gospels tell us this was the same Mary who anointed the Lord with ointment and wiped his feet with her hair (John 11:1–2). John is referring here to the story in Luke of the dinner at the house of Simon the leper in the same town of Bethany:

> When he arrived at the Pharisee's house and took his place at table, suddenly a woman came in, who had a bad name in the town. She had heard that he was dining with the Pharisee and had brought with her an alabaster jar of ointment. She waited behind him at his feet, weeping, and her tears fell on his feet, and she wiped them away with her hair; then she covered his feet with kisses and anointed them with the ointment. (Luke 7:36–47)

The story ends with the beautiful and consoling words of Jesus: "For this reason I tell you that her sins, many as they are, have been forgiven her, because she has shown such great love. It is someone who is forgiven little who shows little love" (Luke 7:47). Again in Luke (10:38–42) we are told the story of Martha inviting Jesus into her home and becoming jealous of Mary "who sat at the Lord's feet and listened to him speaking," while she was busy about many things. ▼ The most striking passage portraying the deep affection that existed between Jesus and Mary and Martha occurs in the story of the resurrection of Lazarus, their brother, from the dead. "Mary went to Jesus, and as soon as she saw him she threw herself at his feet, saying, 'Lord, if you had been here, my brother would not have died.' At the sight of her tears . . . Jesus was greatly distressed, and with a profound sigh he said, 'Where have you put him?'" (John 11:32–34). ▼ A second anointing just before Jesus' death is recounted by John (12:1–3): "Six days before the Passover, Jesus went to Bethany, where Lazarus was, whom he had raised from the dead. They gave a dinner for him there; Martha waited on them and Lazarus was among those at table. Mary brought in a pound of very costly ointment, pure nard, and with it anointed the feet of Jesus, wiping them with her hair; the house was filled with the scent of the ointment." ▼ We should note that Jesus' family of choice was far from the traditional Jewish family. First of all, they were a family of three unmarried adults living together. This must have been unusual since Jewish law required that all Jews marry and procreate. Second we are told that Mary "had a bad name in town"; but we are not told what her many sins were. Although Mary and Martha are referred to as "sisters" and Lazarus is referred to as their "brother," we should note that frequently in the Bible the words sister and brother are used not to designate a biological relationship but to recognize a deep committed love relationship. ▼ This leaves open the possibility that Jesus' family of choice was a gay family; that Mary and Martha were lesbians and Lazarus a gay man. In any case Jesus' choice of family was not limited to the conventional and his value judgment had to do with the quality of love that united the members, rather than their gender or sexual orientation. I am personally convinced that, if Jesus were among us today, he might well choose to befriend a loving lesbian or gay couple and seek their company.

Scriptural Charter for the Inclusion of Lesbians and Gays

There is one passage in Scripture that I believe prophetically indicates that the Spirit of God is poured out in a special way on all those gay and lesbian Christians who are sincerely seeking to live their lives according to the teachings of Christ. This is the account of the baptism of the Ethiopian eunuch in the Acts of the Apostles (8:26–39). The Lucan author's purpose is to depict the work of the Holy Spirit in the formation of the first Christian community, and how that community differed from its predecessor. He stresses that people who were considered outcasts by Israel for various reasons were to be included in the new community. One of these groups, symbolized by the eunuch, are those who for sexual reasons were excluded from the Old Testament community. "A man whose testicles have been crushed or whose adult male member has been cut off must not be admitted to the assembly of Yahweh" (Deut. 23:2). ▼ However, in Isaiah (56:3–8), there is an explicit prophesy that, with the coming of the Messiah and the establishment of the new covenant, the eunuch, who was for-

merly excluded from the community of God, will be given a
special place in the Lord's house and an immortal name:

> No foreigner adhering to Yahweh
>   should say, "Yahweh will utterly
>   exclude me
>   from his people."
> No eunuch should say, "Look, I am a
>   dried tree."
> For Yahweh says this:
>   "To the eunuchs who observe my
>   Sabbaths,
> and choose to do my good pleasure
> and cling to my covenant,
> I shall give them in my house
>   and within my walls
> a monument and a name
>   better than sons and daughters;
> I shall give them an everlasting name
> that will never be effaced
> . . . .
> these I shall lead to my holy mountain,
> and make them joyful
>   in my house of prayer.
> Their burnt offerings and sacrifices
>   will be accepted on my altar,
> for my house will be called
>   a house of prayer for all peoples."
> Lord Yahweh
>   who gathers the exiles of Israel
>   declares:

"There are others I shall gather
besides those already gathered."

This prophesy includes the homosexual because the term "eunuch" in the New Testament is used not only in its literal sense, to mean those who have been physically castrated, but also in a symbolic sense, for all those who do not marry and bear children. For example, in Matthew (19:12), Jesus, discussing marriage and divorce, says to his apostles: "There are eunuchs born so from their mother's womb, there are eunuchs made so by human agency and there are eunuchs who have made themselves so for the sake of the kingdom of Heaven."

▼ The first category, that of eunuchs who have been so from birth, is the closest description we have in the Bible of what we understand today as a person with a homosexual orientation. It should come as no surprise then, that one of the first groups of outcasts of Israel that the Holy Spirit includes within the new covenant community is symbolized by the Ethiopian eunuch. Note that it is the Holy Spirit that takes the initiative by leading Philip to the encounter with the Ethiopian eunuch, who is treasurer of the Court of the Queen of Ethiopia. The eunuch, as was his practice, had made a pilgrimage to the temple of Jerusalem, and spent his time there in prayer to Yahweh. As he was riding home along the road to Jericho, he was reading Isaiah, who predicts that after the Messiah comes there will be a special place in the house of the Lord for eunuchs who in place of progeny will be given immortal life in heaven.

He was now on his way home; and as he sat in his chariot he was reading the prophet Isaiah. The Spirit said to Philip,

"Go up and join that chariot." When Philip ran up, he heard him reading Isaiah the prophet and asked, "Do you understand what you are reading?" He replied, "How could I, unless I have someone to guide me?" So he urged Philip to get in and sit by his side. Now the passage of scripture he was reading was this:

Like a lamb led to the slaughterhouse,
    like a sheep dumb in front of its
    shearers,
he never opens his mouth.
In his humiliation
    fair judgement was denied him.
Who will ever talk about his
    descendants,
since his life on earth has been
    cut short?

The eunuch addressed Philip and said, "Tell me, is the prophet referring to himself or someone else?" Starting, therefore, with this text of scripture Philip proceeded to explain the good news of Jesus to him.

Further along the road they came to some water, and the eunuch said, "Look, there is some water here; is there anything to prevent my being baptized?" He ordered the chariot to stop, then Philip

and the eunuch both went down into the
water and he baptised him. But after they
had come up out of the water again Philip
was taken away by the Spirit of the Lord,
and the eunuch never saw him again but
went on his way rejoicing. (Acts 8:28–39)

The eunuch rides on into history "full of joy." I like to
think of this eunuch as the first baptized gay Christian. It should
be obvious that we are dealing here not just with the story of an
individual. The symbolism of the passage is quite obvious. The
Holy Spirit takes the initiative in leading the new Christian community to include among its members those who were excluded
for sexual reasons from the Old Testament community. Now
that the Messiah has come there no longer is a need for every
member of that community to procreate in the hope of father-
ing the Messiah. ▼ Paul speaks of the Holy Spirit breaking
down all divisions that separate the human family one from
another. Here the Holy Spirit prophetically takes the initiative
to break down the division of gay and straight. We have the
good fortune to live in an age when that prophesy is being fulfilled by the gay liberation movement which is a continuation
of the initiative of the Holy Spirit. We can accept that eunuch of
the court of the Queen of Ethiopia as our first gay Christian
brother in Christ and the apostle Philip as our special patron.
And the judgment of the Spirit of God Him/Herself stands for
all time: *There is no reason why those who are sexually different cannot be received as fully qualified members into the
Christian community!* ▼ We can conclude with certainty after recalling these four gay-positive episodes in the New Testament that homosexuality has not been condemned by the
Church because Jesus condemned it, but because the Church

inherited a condemnation of homosexuality from a world-view, expressed in many if not all cultures, which did not understand homosexuality and feared that which was different. The same question is before the Church today as was before John the Evangelist: Are we ready to go forward in faith, overcoming the death-dealing attitude of the world which has *"exchanged God's truth* for a lie and [has] worshipped and served the creature instead of the Creator"* (Rom. 1:25) or will we let stand hate, fear, and ignorance of lesbian women and gay men who are our sisters and brothers in Christ? Will we deny them the place which Christ evidently found for them in his proclamation of the Good News, or will we as a faith community seek to overcome our fears and prejudices, so long influenced by those of the world, to embrace the love and freedom of the Gospel, which reaches forth to embrace all people?

▼

CHAPTER 12

GOD'S LOVE *of* GAYS

The people that walked in darkness
    have seen a great light;
on the inhabitants of a country
    in shadow dark as death
    light has blazed forth.
                    Isaiah 9: 1

If any of you suffer, as I do, from the psychic phenomenon referred to as SAD, which I like to decipher as "seasonal adjustment depression," you are very sensitive each winter to the great war going on in nature between night and day, darkness and light. At the time of the winter solstice which occurs right before Christmas, darkness seems to be winning the battle; we have the longest nights and the shortest days of the year. And if it were not for the fact that we are celebrating the joyous birthday feast of Jesus, the new light of the world, my winter depression could easily grow into a serious crisis. But each day after the winter solstice, daylight increases and night diminishes, annually renewing the hope in my spirit that light will gradually replace darkness outside of me and hope will replace despair inside of me. And finally, by the spring equinox, which occurs right around Easter, days start becoming longer than nights. By the summer solstice, light has conquered darkness and, at least for a brief period, we seem to have endless days and brief nights. During these long summer days it is relatively easy for the light of resurrection hope to have victory over the darkness of despair.

Saint John, the disciple whom Jesus loved, also uses the symbol of Jesus Christ as the light of the world in the Prologue of his gospel:

> *In the beginning was the Word:*
> *the Word was with God*
> *and the Word was God.*
> *He was with God in the beginning.*
> *Through him all things came into being,*
> *not one thing came into being*
> *   except through him.*
> *What has come into being in him was life,*
> *life that was the light of men;*
> *and light shines in darkness,*
> *and darkness could not overpower it. (John 1:1–5)*

Deep in our psyche as gay men and lesbian women there is another war between night and day, light and darkness, between the voices that would like to plunge our spirit into the darkness of self-rejection and despair and the voice of love that strives to bring the light of hope, peace, and joy into our spirit. In this chapter I will discuss the great love that exists between God and gay and lesbian people, the reason for hope in our lives. What I say here is inspired by Henri Nouwen, in my opinion one of the best writers on the spiritual life in our day. His twenty-fifth book, *Life of the Beloved: Spiritual Living in a Secular World*, is a ringing affirmation that everyone is loved by God and can enjoy "the life of the beloved."[1]

Nouwen begins by retelling the events that followed on Jesus' baptism as recounted in Matthew (3:16–17): "And when Jesus had been baptised he at once came up from the water, and suddenly the heavens opened and he saw the Spirit of God descending like a dove and coming down on him. And suddenly there was a voice from heaven, 'This is my Son, the Beloved; my favour rests on him.'"

These words of God are spoken to everyone of us, and, I believe, in a special way to those of us who are God's lesbian daughters and gay sons. They were spoken and continue to be spoken at our creation. Each one of us in our unique existential reality are the ongoing terminus of a creative act of love from God.

God, from the beginning of time, saw that our lesbian or gay reality is good and through a unique act of love willed us into being. We must remember that God does not create as a human artist creates. God does not will us into being and then forgets us. If God were to forget us, we would cease to be. At every moment, the Spirit of God is birthing us out of love. It is this truth about our relationship with God that led all the great mystics and practitioners of centering prayer to go within themselves and seek to experience in the depths of their being the very act by which their being emerges from a loving act of God.

We must recall also that at our baptism in "water and the Spirit" that same voice that thundered from heaven at the baptism of Jesus speaks quietly in our hearts: "You are my beloved lesbian daughter; you are my beloved gay son and I am well pleased in you!" (It is interesting to note that in ancient times the dove was the symbol of Aphrodite, the goddess of love and creation.) At our baptism we were reborn and became sharers of divine life with Jesus. Consequently, whatever God, our Father and Mother, said to Jesus is also said to us. As Paul says: ". . . what you received was not the spirit of slavery to bring you back into fear; you received the Spirit of adoption, enabling us to cry out, 'Abba, Father!'" (Rom. 8:14–15).

"You are the Beloved!" It is my hope for all of you that you can hear God speak these words to you in your heart with all the tenderness and force that love can hold; that these words, whether whispered softly in your heart or thundered loudly from without, will change your night into day, your despair into hope.

It is certainly not always easy for gays to hear that voice, since we live in a world that is filled with voices that shout at us, "You are nobody! You are unlovable!" and in the immortal words of Daffy Duck, "You are despicable!" These negative voices are so loud and so persistent that it is easy to internalize them and begin to believe in them.

As Nouwen points out, the greatest trap in our life, especially, I would add, in our life as gay persons, is not the trap of success, popularity, power, or pleasure. Rather, that trap is self-rejection, the belief that in our very essence we are unlovable and unloved. Jesus came to save us from every form of alienation from ourselves, especially alienation from our body and its sexual feelings. The fundamental message of the Bible concerning our human sexuality is that God placed our sexual power in human hands to be used for appropriate human purposes. As Sebastian Moore points out in his *Jesus: The Liberator of Desire*, Adam and Eve are portrayed in Genesis as being ashamed of their mortal bodies and their sexuality.[2] They wanted to disembody themselves and become pure spirits like God, no longer subject to death. To redeem us from that sin, the Word became flesh and the Word's first miracle was the creation of hundreds of gallons of wine to help celebrate the marriage feast of Cana.

When the voices of darkness prevail and we come to believe that we are worthless and unlovable, then success, popularity, power, and pleasure are easily perceived as attractive solutions to life. Self-rejection can come disguised as Christian humility. True humility means recognizing our dependence on a parental God who loves us; it does not mean rejecting ourselves to escape the anger of a God we fear. Nouwen points out how amazed he is at how quickly he can fall into this temptation: "As soon as someone accuses me or criticizes me; as soon as I am rejected, left alone or abandoned, I find myself thinking I am a nobody. I tend to blame myself, not just for what I did, but for *who I am*. My dark side says: 'I am no good. I deserved to be pushed aside, forgotten, rejected or abandoned. There is nothing lovable about me. I feel covered with shame.'"[3]

Shameful feelings are aroused in us most intensely when we see ourselves as violating in some way the most basic values with which we identify. Healthy shame comes when we act in a way we believe to be wrong, especially if we see that action as mean or destructive. When we repent of those actions and seek forgiveness for them, we restore our psyche to spiritual health. Shame becomes psychologically dangerous, however, when it begins to color our most basic ideas of who we are and how worthy we are. Pathological shame takes the form of self-loathing and self-hatred, and it is always destructive of our ability to grow and develop into our full humanness both psychologically and spiritually. The deepest meaning of the passion and death of Jesus is that he freely entered into and shared our shame and guilt, and by so doing won us freedom.

The self-rejection that arises out of feelings of shame is the greatest enemy of our spiritual life because it contradicts the voice that speaks within us and calls us the "beloved." Being the "beloved" expresses the core truth of our existence. Feelings of shame and self-rejection can lead us to refuse to hear the voice that speaks from the very depth of our being. That voice has been there from creation and was renewed and intensified at baptism; but it seems that I am always much more tuned into and eager to listen to the louder voices of darkness saying: "Prove yourself; prove you are worth something. Do something relevant, spectacular, or powerful, and then you will earn the love you so desire." Even Jesus was tempted this way.

Meanwhile, that soft, gentle voice that speaks in the silence and the solitude of my heart remains unheard or, at least, unconvincing. Many other positive voices come to me in countless ways, voices of parents, lovers, friends, assuring me that I am loved. But all these assurances of love are not sufficient to convince me that I am the beloved. Many of us who are gay feel all our lives that we are living out the life of a false self. Beneath all our confidence and success there remains the question: If all those who claim they love me could see me and know me in my innermost self, would they still love me? That question is a clear indication of how deep the darkness of self-rejection lies. It is similar in spirit to the famous saying attributed to Groucho Marx: "I wouldn't want to belong to any club that would accept me as a member!" That agonizing question rooted in my inner darkness keeps tormenting me. To avoid that agonizing question, I adopt a busy life full of activity and run away from the prayerful silence where the quiet voice calling me "the Beloved" can be heard.

As Elizabeth Johnson points out in her book, *She Who Is: The Mystery of God in Feminist Theological Discourse*, "Insofar as the experience of self is profoundly intertwined with the experience of God, growth or diminishment in one conditioning the other, women's awakening to their own full human worth is a new event in the religious history of humankind. It occasions an experience of God as beneficent toward the female and an ally of woman's flourishing."[4] The same is true in a not unconnected way with gays. For us too, the experience of the gay self is profoundly intertwined with the experience of God. As long as we have internalized a negative, homophobic self-image, our image of God will be an image of a god of fear, guilt, and shame. Perfect love, Scripture tells us, casts out all fear.

Over the past twenty-five years, a gay-positive image has emerged from the heart of the world. Gay spiritual groups have sprung up all over the globe. This is the work of the Holy Spirit and we who are gay should be intensely grateful to God to be alive at this *kairos*, this special time, and to be able to participate in this creative work of the Spirit of God. Since gay liberation, a gay-positive experience of ourselves and our loving relationships can give rise to a whole new and healthy experience of God as a loving God who accepts us and affirms us in our gayness and in the love of our gay relationships. Great images of the divine, Martin Buber observed, come into being not simply as a projection of the imagination, but as an awakening from the deep abyss of human existence in a real encounter with divine power and glory.[5] Images with the capacity to evoke the divine are given in encounters that, at the same time, bring persons to birth as persons, as Thou's, in reciprocal relation with the Eternal Thou. I believe that just as women's liberation has resulted in new feminist understandings of God, so too, the experience of gay liberation is resulting in a whole new set of homoerotic metaphors for our relationship with God to complement the heteroerotic metaphors of tradition.

In a parallel way with women's liberation, lesbians and gays are newly involved in experiencing and articulating themselves as active subjects and good ones in history. Given the negative assessment of lesbian and gay humanity under homophobic and heterosexist patriarchy, this self-assertion has the character of a conversion process, a turning away from the self-rejection of oneself as gay and a turning toward one's gay self as worthwhile, as in fact a gift, in community with many others making the same discovery of their worth.

Gays are going through a rebirth that is accomplished in a

dialectic of contrast and confirmation. First there is the experience of homophobia interpreted consciously as hateful oppression. The hateful voices of night and darkness have recently reached a crescendo, filling the headlines, the television and radio talk shows. As President Clinton announced his intention to lift the ban on gays in the military, the Joint Chiefs of Staff fought that action by claiming that gays would "destroy morale, undermine discipline, force devoutly religious service members to resign and increase the risk of AIDS for heterosexual troops." The Ancient Order of Hibernians, a fraternal group that sponsors the annual St. Patrick day parade in New York City, announced that they will not march with openly gay Irish because what they are represents sin. The Council of Churches denied "observer" status to Metropolitan Community Church, the fastest growing church in the world, because being gay is seen as contrary to God's law as revealed in Scripture. The State of Colorado denied all civil rights to gays after a campaign of lies and defamation by the religious right. The Cardinal of New York called all the state government representatives and urged them to defeat a gay rights bill because it could lead to approving an immoral life-style. A recent Vatican statement urged the European Parliament not to recognize the right of gays to legal marriage or to adopt children. Fundamentalists have proclaimed that AIDS is God's just judgment on us because of our sinful life. But these external voices of darkness will have no hold on us, unless they can join a voice of self-rejection within.

We have a desperate need, then, to receive the grace from God for a conversion experience. The many-faceted dehumanization into which we gays are cast comes into consciousness through struggle against it and shared, prayerful thought about it. One of the best ways to heal our wounds is in the context of a lesbian and gay community of prayer. This combination of praxis and reflection has led many in the gay community into a deep sense of indignation. And this indignation in turn has led to a deep sense of community among lesbians and gays, an awakening of hope that things can be different.

As we have seen, conversion has a radically different meaning for women and implies conversion to self-esteem, rather than away from it. This is doubly true for gay people who are told that what they are is sinful and that their conversion involves self-rejection. Gays who interiorize self-rejection turn over the power of self-definition to their enemies. The primordial temptation of lesbians and gays is not to pride and self-assertion, but rather to a lack of it, to a diffusion of a personal center, over-dependence on others for a self-identity, drifting and fear of recognizing one's own competence. Conversion involves turning away from an interiorized homophobic identity toward new ownership of the gay self as God's good gift. We must never let ourselves be defined by those who hate us; we can only be defined by that interior voice that calls us the "beloved."

A similar distinction should be made concerning the use of the word ego. This word has completely opposite connotations in classical spirituality and in psychotherapy. Freud provided us with two formulations that indicate the direction and aim of healthy psychic growth: first, "to make the unconscious conscious" or second, and more fully, "Wo es war soll ich werden." This can be translated literally as: "Where it was, let the I become"; where "it" signifies the impersonal and "I" signifies the personal.[6] These formulations imply a conception of human nature: promoting the individual's consciousness, fostering ego development, taking responsibility for oneself and one's unconscious. The *soll* or "shall" indicates the setting of a goal for growth. The idea of responsibility in its most basic sense refers to the ability of the I or self to transpose the chaos of raw experience and interior drives of the id onto a meaningful plane. To express this in theological terms: we can, out of our freedom, be co-creators of our very self in cooperation with the divine spirit. The original translators of Freud's work chose to translate *es* and *ich* in more esoteric terms than "it" and "I," so they chose the latin words *id* and *ego*. "Ego" then became the name of the authentic, free, conscious self and strengthening the ego became the goal of psychic health.

The word ego has exactly the opposite meaning in most spiritual tradition. In Western Christian tradition, the word "ego" was used to indicate the prideful self that will not acknowledge any dependence on others or on the divine. In a similar vein, Heinz Kohut, in his book *How Does Analysis Cure?*, rejects the idea of total autonomy as the goal of therapy, arguing that the healthy self always needs the sustaining response of objects that respond directly to the self from the first to the last breath.[7] Kohut includes God among those objects we depend on. In

Eastern spiritual tradition, the ego usually refers to the illusion of a separate self that stands in the way of enlightenment.

For most gay people, having a strong and healthy ego in the Freudian sense of the term is, I believe, essential to having a healthy and mature spiritual life. We must first work to achieve a secure self-identity before we can begin the spiritual process of freely letting go of it in order to become one with the transcending Spirit of God.

Personal development in our understanding of the self also constitutes development of our experience of God; loss of a positive self-identity is also loss of a positive experience of God. Consequently, when one claims the self in freedom, or finds a new way of loving others and thus, oneself, or affirms oneself in trustful acceptance, then the changing history of this self-revelation also entails living through a changing history of the experience of God. Most gay and lesbian believers discover that their conversion, experienced not as giving up oneself but as tapping into the power of one's self, simultaneously releases understanding of divine power not as dominating power-over but as the passionate ability to empower ourselves and others. Our God, Blondel wrote, lies within us; and the only way to become one with our God is to become one with our authentic self.

We lesbians and gays must, then, listen to that inner voice of God with great inner attentiveness, tuning out all negative, hateful voices. When, from a positive self-image, you listen to God's voice speaking within you these are the kinds of words you will hear:

> I have called you by name from the very beginning.
> You are mine and I am yours. You are my beloved; on
> you my favor rests. I have molded you in the depths of
> the earth and knitted you together in your mother's
> womb. I have carved you in the palm of my hand and
> hidden you in the shadow of my embrace. I look at you
> with infinite tenderness and care for you with a care
> more intimate than that of a mother with her child.
> I have counted every hair of your head and guide you
> at every step. Wherever you go, I go with you, and
> wherever you rest, I keep watch. I will give you food

*that will satisfy all your hunger, and water that
quenches your thirst. I will not hide my face from you.
You know me as your own, and I know you as my own.
You belong to me. I am your father, and mother, your
brother, your sister, your lover, your spouse; yes, even
your child.*[8]

CHAPTER 13

The SPECIAL NATURE

of the GAY *and* LESBIAN

LOVE *of* GOD

Blessed is anyone who trusts in Yahweh, with Yahweh
to rely on. Such a person is like a tree by the waterside
that thrusts its roots to the stream . . .
Jeremiah 17:7–8

After reflecting on the special love that God has for lesbians
and gays, I would like to reflect here on the special kind of love gays and
lesbians can have for God. As I become what the Irish like to call "long
in the tooth," I particularly like this passage from Jeremiah. Woody Al-
len once quipped that the only difference between a believer and an atheist is that the believer has "hidden assets." I visualize that hidden asset
as a taproot sunk into the deep-down waters of God's love. So come what
may—tempest, drought, old age, illness—we can remain green, viable,
and growing with hope and love.

We are told that St. John, the disciple whom Jesus loved,
was the longest surviving companion of Jesus. Young converts to Christ
would come to him and ask, "Is there any action or saying of Jesus that
you remember that has not been recorded?" John would respond, "Little

children, Jesus had only one message: 'Love one another as I have loved you!' " The poet William Blake once said, "We were put here on earth for a little space to bear the beams of love!" As I grow older the only topic I want to write about is the transcendent love affair of my life, the love affair with God.

We gay people need to realize that it is God who has risked the first approach and made Him/Herself vulnerable to our acceptance or rejection. "Let us love, then, because he first loved us."(1 John 4:19). God is an intensely jealous lover but has created us free and has enormous respect for our freedom. God offers us His/Her love but awaits our free response. We need to open ourselves to the full import of these words of God: "I have called you by your name, you are mine. . . . I regard you as precious . . . you are honored and I love you . . ." (Isa. 43: 1–4). I believe this is the only place in all scripture where those three words, "I love you," are spoken directly to us by God.

As gay men and lesbians, it is important for us to realize that if we intend to have an intense love relation with God, we must pray the way we love. All the great mystics imaged their love relationship with God in erotic images. The most important example of this is the Old Testament book *The Song of Songs* which talks about a human's spiritual relationship with God in intensely erotic language: "The flash of it is a flash of fire, a flame of Yahweh himself" (8:6).

If I am a gay man and image God as male, or if I am a lesbian and image God as female, then there is a necessary homoerotic dimension of my prayer relationship with God. If I hate and despise my homoerotic feelings out of an interiorized homophobia, I am incapable of a deep and passionate love relationship with God. I then can relate only to an abstract god of rules and authority, the god of pathology, the god of fear, shame, and guilt.

For most gay and lesbian people, it is the human experience of gay love that opens the door of hope to the possibility of a passionate love relationship with God. As Patrick Arnold observes in his book *Wildmen, Warriors and Kings: Masculine Spirituality in the Bible*, "Falling in love is the most important clue a human can ever find to his or her latent spiritual needs and potentialities. Without this experience a human's relationship with God remains largely one of obedience, respect and will, but one that ultimately lacks passion, heart and love."[1] As St.

Augustine is reported to have said: "Show me a human in love, and I'll show you a human on the way to God."

The ultimate drive in the human psyche toward the intimacy of love is a built-in drive toward oneness with the infinite reality of God Him/Herself. Although our human loves are good in themselves and open us up to our longing for the divine, our human loves can never fill up the capacity in us for loving intimacy. The spiritual gay or lesbian will gradually come to recognize that, in the intensity of their erotic infatuation, they have confused and transferred onto another human being the real desires and genuine needs that only one love can fulfill and that love is God. Again in the words of St. Augustine: "You have made us for yourself, oh my God, and our hearts will never rest until they rest in you."

The great spiritual leaders of the past have always taught that God in fact nurtures our growth in capacity and potential for a passionate intimate relationship with God. Saint Gregory of Nyssa, for example, describes beautifully the step-by-step nature of spiritual growth. He says that God waits on our freedom. Our first serious "yes" to God enables divine love to begin to act within us. Our inner space, as a result of that "yes," is then ready to receive something of God. God fills that space as fully as we are able to accept. At the same time, this filling enlarges the space, and we long for more. Thus, the lover of God is always filled to his or her capacity, and always longs for more of God. Yet the longing does not bring frustration because there is a fullness. According to St. Gregory, this process goes on beyond death into infinity because God is infinite. For all eternity, we continue to grow deeper and deeper in union with a God who is infinite and, therefore, can never be exhausted.

We are called, then, to a loving intimacy with an infinite God. The greatest obstacle to undertaking this spiritual journey can be fear. Our God would prefer a thousand mistakes in the extravagance of love to any paralysis in the caution of fear.

We must open ourselves then to a love affair with God. Invite God into a deep and passionate homoerotic relationship! Get in touch with the burning desire deep in your heart for union with the divine. Listen to the passionate sensuality of this prayer of love to God by Augustine:

*Late have I loved you, O Beauty ever ancient, ever
new; late have I loved you! You were within me, but
I was outside, and it was there that I searched for you.
In my unloveliness I plunged into the lovely things
which you created. You were with me, but I was not
with you. Created things kept me from you; yet if they
had not been in you they would not have been at all.
You called, you shouted, and you broke through my
deafness. You flashed, you shone, and you dispelled my
blindness. You breathed your fragrance on me; I drew
in breath and now I pant for you. I have tasted you,
now I hunger and thirst for more. You touched me,
and now I burn for your peace.*[2]

Make God your primary love object. Write love letters and
poems to God. Listen to these following love poems to God written by
my friend Samuel Menashe:

*O Many Named Beloved
Listen to my praise
Various as the seasons
Different as the days
All my treasons cease
When I see your face*

*The silence is vast
I am still and wander
Keeping you in mind
There is never enough time
To know another*[3]

Invite God into a dance. When I was a young man, God
would let me take the lead, but now that I am older, God takes the lead.
Make your own these words of Psalm 57 (ll. 7–8):

*My heart is ready, God,
   my heart is ready;*

I will sing, and make music for you.
  Awake, my glory,
awake, lyre and harp,
  that I may awake the Dawn.

I like to imagine God as dressed all in white, looking remarkably like John Travolta, and inviting me to dance, while the Bee Gees in the background sing, "Ooo! Ooo! Ooo! Ooo! Staying alive! Staying alive!"

E P I L O G U E

EMERGING *from the*

HEART *of the* WORLD

Twenty-five years ago, in 1968, the gay Christian movement began as a visible, organized presence in the human community, with the creation of Metropolitan Community Church, followed two years later by the founding of Dignity and many other Christian gay groups. In his preface to the French translation of *Taking a Chance on God*, Father Jacques Perotti, a leader in the Christian gay movement in France, speaks of this new era as a *declic*, a special moment in history, "a revelation of the slow emergence of a positive homosexual identity from the heart of the world. After so many ages of rejection, destruction and intimidation, a wind of freedom began to blow."[1] I am convinced that gay liberation is a central part of the great dialectic of human liberation that God is working out through His/Her holy spirit. In this epilogue, I will describe that dialectic and the special role that gays and lesbians have to play in that dialectic. Scripture tells us, "Without a vision the people will perish!" Gay people have a special need for a vision of their role in bringing about the reign of God in history to sustain them in the difficult battles that lie ahead. I will begin with a broad vision of the dialectic of human liberation, and then describe how the gay spiritual liberation movement fits into that dialectic.

My overview owes a great debt to the book *The Passion of the Western Mind: Understanding the Ideas that Have Shaped Our World View* by Richard Tarnas.[2] I have a great love of philosophy; one of my philosophy professors once called me *homo naturaliter metaphysicus*. I found this book by Tarnas, who is a philosopher and an intellectual historian, to be one of the most brilliant books in the field that I have ever read. Tarnas deals with the interplay of philosophy, religion, and science in the evolutionary development of Western culture over the past three thousand years.

Tarnas's basic insight is that the period of the past three thousand years in the development of philosophy, science, religion, and culture has been an exclusively male phenomenon from start to finish. Western intellectual tradition has been produced and canonized almost totally by men: Socrates, Plato, Aristotle, Jesus, Paul, Augustine, Aquinas, Luther, Copernicus, Galileo, Bacon, Descartes, Newton, Locke, Hume, Kant, Darwin, Blondel, Marx, Nietzsche, Freud, Buber, and so on.

According to Tarnas, the masculinity of the Western mind has been pervasive and fundamental in both men and women, affecting every aspect of Western thought, determining its most basic conception of the human being and the human role in the world. All the major languages within which the Western tradition has developed have tended to personify the human species with words that are masculine in gender. It was only twenty to twenty-five years ago that our culture became consciously aware that the only words we had for all humankind were words that were masculine: *anthropos, homo, l'homme, el hombre, l'uomo, chelovek, der Mensch, man*. In the past, the word "man" was felt to be uniquely capable of indicating a metaphorically singular and personal entity who is also intrinsically collective in character, a universal individual.

> *As a close reading of the many relevant texts—Greco-Roman, Judeo-Christian and modern scientific-humanistic—makes clear, both the syntactical structure and the essential meaning of the language that most major Western thinkers have used to represent the*

human condition and the human enterprise; including
its drama, its pathos and its hubris are intrinsically
associated with the archetypal figure "man."[3]

Within this cultural context, suppressing the feminine in themselves, men tended to feel superior to women. Most women, in turn, not being able to repress the feminine, interiorized feelings of inferiority and inadequacy that they derived from the culture.

Tarnas makes the point that when gender-biased language is no longer the established norm, the entire cultural worldview will have moved into a new era. The old kinds of sentences and phrases, the character of the human self-image, the place of humanity in the cosmos and its nature, the very nature of the human drama, all will have been radically transformed. "As the language goes, so goes the worldview—and vice versa."[4]

By archetype, Tarnas is referring to Jung's conception of the archetypes as autonomous patterns of meaning that appear to structure and inhere in both psyche and matter, thereby in effect dissolving the modern subject-object dichotomy. The relation of the human mind to the world is ultimately not dualistic but participatory. Those *a priori* forms that govern the development of the human psyche are in effect the same forms that guide and direct the evolution of the world. As the progress of modern subjective philosophy cut the link between the human mind and objective structures of reality:

> *Jung, under the impact of far more powerful and extensive experiences of the human psyche, both his own and others, pushed the Kantian and Freudian perspectives all the way, until he reached a kind of holy grail of the inner quest: the discovery of the universal archetypes in all their power and rich complexity as the fundamental determining structures of human experience.*[5]

The archetypally patterned collective unconscious was the primordial foundation of the psyche itself and is at the same time the law of the development of the universe.

Tarnas drew his primary evidence for an archetypal dialectic in the human psyche from Stanislav Grof's analysis of the reliving of the experience of biological birth. The archetypal sequence that governed these perinatal phenomena from womb through birth canal to birth is experienced above all as a powerful dialectic—moving from an initial state of undifferentiated unity to a problematic state of constriction, conflict, and contradiction with an accompanying sense of separation, duality, and alienation to an unexpected redemptive liberation that both overcomes and fulfills the intervening alienated state—restoring the initial unity but on a new level that preserves the achievement of the whole trajectory.[6]

This archetypal dialectic, Tarnas claims, is experienced simultaneously on an individual level and, often more powerfully, a collective level, so that the movement from primordial unity through alienation to liberating resolution is experienced in terms of the evolution of an entire culture or of humankind as a whole—the birth of *Homo sapiens* out of nature no less than the birth of the individual child from the mother. "Here personal and transpersonal were equally present, inextricably fused, so that ontogeny [the development of an individual organism] not only recapitulated phylogeny [the evolution of a whole kind or type of organism] but in some sense opened out into it."[7]

The archetypal dialectic according to Tarnas is experienced in several dimensions: physical, psychological, intellectual, and spiritual. In *physical* terms, this is the dialectic of the birth experience described above.

In *psychological* terms, the experience is one of movement from an initial condition of undifferentiated pre-ego consciousness to a state of increasing individuation and separation between self and world, increasing existential alienation, and finally an experience of ego death followed by psychological rebirth; this is often complexly associated with the biographical experience of moving from the womb of childhood through the labor of life and the contraction of aging to the encounter with death.

On the *religious* level, especially frequent was the Judeo-Christian symbolic movement from the primordial Garden through the Fall, the exile into separation from the divinity, into the world of suf-

fering and mortality, followed by the redemptive crucifixion and resurrection, bringing the reunion of the divine and the human.

Finally, on the *philosophical* level, the experience is compre-
hensible as a dialectical evolution from an archetypally structured primordial Unity, through an emanation into matter with increasing com-
plexity, multiplicity, and individuation, through a state of absolute
alienation, followed by a dramatic *Aufhebung*, a synthesis and reunifi-
cation with self-subsistent Being that both annihilates and fulfills the
individual trajectory.

The evolution of the Western mind, Tarnas notes, is marked
at every step by a complex interplay of masculine and feminine. There
was a significant partial reunion with the feminine corresponding to
every great creative watershed of Western culture, for example, the great
openness to the feminine in the personality of Jesus. Another example
is found in William Meissner's *Ignatius of Loyola: The Psychology of a
Saint*. Meissner identifies the transformation of Ignatius from a soldier
and *bon vivant* to a mystic, a saint, and the founder of a religious order
with his acceptance of the feminine dimension of himself.

> *To a large extent, the feminine aspects of {Ignatius'}
> character play the dominant role in his mysticism, re-
> flected in his yearning for love, his intense affectivity,
> his passivity and submissive yielding to the divine em-
> brace, and the overwhelming experience of copious tears
> to the point of physical disability. I have suggested
> that at some level his mystical absorption may have its
> psychic roots in the yearning of the abandoned child
> for its lost mother.*[8]

Meissner finds an interesting parallel in the psychic dynamics that underlay Ignatius' conversion and the artistic creation of his contemporary Michelangelo Buonarroti:

> *The parallels of Michelangelo with Ignatius are
> striking, but for Ignatius the creative resolution of the
> deep-seated unconscious conflict and its related fantasy
> took the form of mystical ecstasy rather than artistic*

externalization. The god-representation in his inner world became the restitutive substitute for his lost mother and fulfilled part of the deeper longing. The pattern of similarity between Ignatius and Michelangelo extends even to an identification with the lost mother that underlies the apparent maternal qualities of both men. For Michelangelo, this resolution took a homosexual form that led to his adopting a maternal role with beautiful young men in sexual liaisons that were equivalently efforts to master the effects of early maternal deprivation. For Ignatius, this aspect of the resolution took the more sublimated form of a religiously tinged paternity and an Eriksonian generativity permeated by the nurturant and maternal qualities derived from his identification with the lost mother.[9]

The Internal Masculine Dialectic

Tarnas notes, also, that there is an archetypal polarity or dialectic within the masculine itself. On the one hand, the masculine principle (again, in both men and women) involves what can be called the Promethean impulse: restless, heroic, rebellious and revolutionary, individualistic and innovative, eternally seeking freedom, autonomy, change, and the new. On the other hand, there is the Saturnian impulse which is both complement and opposite to the Promethean impulse: conservative, stabilizing, controlling, dominating, that which seeks to sustain, order, contain, and repress. This is the juridical-structural-hierarchical side of the masculine that has expressed itself in patriarchy.

The two sides of the masculine—Prometheus and Saturn, son and father—are implications of each other. Each requires, calls forth, and grows into its opposite. On a broad scale the dynamic tension between these two principles can be seen as constituting the dialectic that propels "history" (political, intellectual, spiritual). It is this dialectic that has driven the internal drama

> *throughout* The Passion of the Western Mind
> *the unceasing dynamic interplay between order and*
> *change, authority and rebellion, control and freedom,*
> *tradition and innovation, structure and revolution. I*
> *am suggesting, however, that this powerful dialectic*
> *ultimately propels and is propelled by—as it were, in*
> *the service of—yet a larger overarching dialectic in-*
> *volving the feminine or "life."*[10]

This development of the masculine archetype with the repression of the feminine, Tarnas assures us, did not occur because women are any less intelligent than men; nor is it due solely to social restrictions placed on women. The "man" of the Western intellectual tradition, as some feminists claim, can be seen as simply a socially constructed "false universal," the use of which both reflected and helped shape a male-dominated society. With this understanding of male domination, some feminists have as their agenda to deconstruct this "socially constructed false male universal" and assert a socially constructed feminine "she" model in its place, replacing man with woman, a father God with a Goddess, the male quest for autonomy and freedom with a feminine quest for symbiosis and merging into the feminine divine matrix.

Tarnas, however, believes that we are dealing today with something much more profound and necessary than a mere substitution. It is my belief that we are dealing here with the *animus/anima mundi*, the Spirit of God, who is working out an evolutionary dialectic. Its past thesis was the development of the masculine archetype which, for some mysterious reason, had to be accomplished first; its present and future antithesis will be the working out of a feminine archetype, which will not contradict or repress the masculine, but eventually result in the synthesis of an androgynous fulfillment of all humans, male and female.

I suspect that the historical priority given to the working out of the masculine archetype had something to do with the greater power and closeness to life and nature of the feminine. If the feminine archetype had been worked out first, the masculine development, which is much more fragile, could never have occurred or taken place only with extreme difficulty. Now we can no more simply return to the divine maternal matrix, than an adult could find fulfillment by returning to the mother's womb.

The "man" of the Western tradition has been a questing hero, a Promethean biological and metaphysical rebel who has constantly sought freedom and progress for himself, and who has thus constantly striven to differentiate himself from and control the matrix out of which he emerged. This Promethean hero has been present in both men and women. The evolution of the Western mind has been driven by a heroic impulse to forge an autonomous, conscious, rational self by separating it from the primordial unity with nature. The result of that process has been the transcendent self, the independent individual ego, the self-determining human being in its existential uniqueness, separateness, and freedom.

This entire book is solidly within that evolutionary process of liberation. The final stage of that masculine liberation into *Freedom, Glorious Freedom* for both men and women has to do with spiritual liberation into an independent stance vis-à-vis the divine and a separation off from a collective identity within the institutional church. Freedom of conscience expresses the direct, unmediated access of the Promethean individual to the divine in a free, direct, and personal relationship of love. The gay liberation process of "coming out of the closet" is another Promethean journey into autonomy and authenticity. Twelve-step spirituality has to do with still another process of liberation from and control over being submerged in addiction of any kind and winning through to personal freedom.

The balancing feminine moment has to do with building a loving gay spiritual community and achieving a deep passionate relationship of personal love with each other and the divine, a relationship built not on any submersion of our ego and identity into any collective or matrix, but built instead on a relationship and a community freely entered into by free, autonomous, independent, and self-determining individuals.

Why, Tarnas asks, has the pervasive masculinity of the Western intellectual and spiritual tradition suddenly become so apparent to us over the past few years, while it remained invisible and unconscious to almost every previous generation? It is only through the feminist movement in the last twenty years that we have become conscious of how exclusively masculine, for example, our common prayers and liturgies were. Hegel once made the observation: "The owl of Minerva spreads her wings only at the falling of dusk!"[11] Every civilization is unconscious of itself, until it reaches its death, and it is only in the dying stages that it becomes fully conscious of what it was all about. True wisdom can only be achieved at the end point. The three-thousand-year masculine tradition of Western civilization is reaching its apogee; it has been pressed to its utmost one-sided extreme in the consciousness of the late modern mind.

The crisis of modern humanity is an essentially masculine crisis. As we have seen, the evolution of the Western mind has been founded on the repression of the feminine, "on the repression of undifferentiated unitary consciousness, of the *participation mystique* with nature, a progressive denial of the *anima mundi*, of the soul of the world, of the community of being, of mystery and ambiguity, of imagination, emotion, instinct, body, nature, women."[12]

Today men and women face the existential crisis of being solitary and mortal conscious egos thrown into an ultimately meaningless and unknowable universe, an environment that is increasingly artificial, mechanistic, fragmented, soulless, and self-destructive. The evolution of the masculine archetype has reached an impasse. If we continue in that one-sided dialectic, the human race faces the real possibility of self-destruction through nuclear warfare or widescale environmental collapse. Humans are feeling progressively isolated, alienated from their communities, from nature, and from each other. Robert Bellah has explored this alienation in *Habits of the Heart*.[13] This separation from the feminine necessarily calls forth a longing for a reunion with that which has been lost. There is an enormous felt need to rediscover and honor the feminine in all its dimensions.

Tarnas believes that the resolution of this crisis is already occurring in the tremendous emergence of the feminine archetype in our culture.[14] He sees this phenomenon as visible in the rise of feminism, the growing empowerment of women, and the widespread opening up to feminine values by both men and women. He sees further evidence of its emergence in the rapid burgeoning of women's scholarship and gender-sensitive perspectives in virtually every intellectual discipline, especially in the fields of theology and spirituality; in the increasing sense of unity with the planet and all forms of nature on it; in the increasing awareness of the ecological and the growing reaction against political and corporate policies supporting the domination and exploitation of the environment; in the growing embrace of the human community and the accelerating collapse of long-standing political and ideological barriers separating the world's people; in the deepening recognition of the value and necessity of partnership, pluralism, and the interplay of many perspectives.

Tarnas finds still further manifestations of the emergence of the feminine archetype, the *anima mundi*, in the widespread urge to reconnect with the body, the emotions, the unconscious, the imagination and intuition; in the new concern with the mystery of childbirth and the dignity of the maternal; in the growing recognition of an immanent intelligence in nature. It can be seen in the increasing appreciation of indigenous and archaic cultural perspectives such as the Native American, African, and ancient European.

On the theological level, Tarnas points to the new awareness of feminine perspectives of the divine; the archeological recovery of the goddess tradition and the contemporary reemergence of goddess worship; the rise of Sophianic or "Wisdom" tradition in Judaeo-Christian theology; the development of feminine spirituality and the widely noted spontaneous upsurge of feminine archetype phenomena in individual dreams and psychotherapy.

He calls our attention as well to the emergence of the feminine in the great wave of interest in New Age phenomena, for example, in the mythological perspective, in esoteric disciplines, in Eastern mysticism, in shamanism, in archetypal and transpersonal psychology, in hermeneutics and other nonobjectivist epistemologies, in scientific theories of the holonomic universe, morphogenetic fields, dissipative structures, chaos theory, systems theory, the ecology of mind, and the participatory universe.

> The deepest passion of the Western Mind has been to reunite with the ground of its being. *The driving impulse of the West's consciousness has been its dialectical quest not only to realize itself, to forge its*

own autonomy, but also, finally, to recover its connec-
tion with the whole, to come to terms with the great
feminine principle in life: to differentiate itself from
but then rediscover and reunite with the feminine,
with the mystery of life, of nature, of soul. And that
reunion can now occur on a new and profoundly dif-
ferent level from that of the primordial unconscious
unity, for the long evolution of human consciousness
has prepared it to be capable at last of embracing the
ground and matrix of its own being freely and con-
sciously. The telos, *the inner direction and goal, of*
the Western mind has been to reconnect with the cosmic
in a mature participation mystique, *to surrender*
itself freely and consciously, in the embrace of a larger
unity that preserves human autonomy while also tran-
scending human alienation.[15]

One interesting manifestation of the feminine archetype
that Tarnas cites was the papal declaration in 1950 of the *Assumptio Ma-*
riae, that the body and soul of Mary, the mother of Jesus, had been taken
up into heaven at the moment of her death, an anticipation of the ultimate resurrection of all the faithful. The role of Mary in Catholicism
has always been to reveal the repressed feminine face of God, the dimensions of mercy, love, compassion, tenderness, and concern. This became especially necessary when the patriarchal image of God the father
was one that evoked fear, guilt, and shame, and when Church authority
had subordinated compassionate love to the law. This image of Mary as
revealing the maternal dimension of God was expressed beautifully in
the popular prayer, the *Memorare*:

Remember, O most gracious Virgin Mary
that never was it known
that anyone who fled to thy protection,
implored thy help, or sought thy intercession
was left unaided.
Inspired by this confidence,
I fly unto thee, O Virgin of Virgins, my mother,

before thee I come, sinful and sorrowful.
O Mother of the Word incarnate.
despise not my petitions,
but in your mercy hear and answer me. Amen.

The symbolism of the Assumption places male and female persons as equals in the domain of heaven.[16]

Many women today, who are more in touch with both their feminine and masculine dimensions, are increasingly unwilling to play the role of being the mediators of the feminine emotional and compassionate needs of men. They are demanding, and rightly so, that we men get deeply in touch with our own feminine dimension. Much of the more positive side of the men's movement has been seeking to open the male psyche to the feminine values of emotions, intuition, compassion. Many men, in turn, who are becoming more in touch with both the masculine and feminine dimensions of themselves, are beginning to refuse to play the role of being the mediators of the masculine needs of women for assertiveness and autonomy. Both genders are being called on to develop the fullness of their own humanity, so they can approach each other as complete, independent persons and not remain essentially dependent on the other gender for their completion.

The Role of Impasse

What is evident about this dialectic is that at every stage and on every level—biological, psychological, and spiritual—the prior process must reach an impasse and undergo a profound and terrifying experience of death in order to achieve this reintegration of the repressed feminine. The masculine must undergo an ego death; the Western mind must be willing to open itself to a reality the nature of which could shatter its most established beliefs about itself and the world. This dialectical advance cannot and will not happen without our cooperation out of our freedom. As Tarnas points out: "This is where the real act of heroism is going to be. What is called for is a courageous act of faith, of imagination, of trust in a larger and more complex reality and an act of unflinching self-discernment."

*This is the great challenge of our time, the evolution-
ary imperative for the masculine to see through and
overcome its hubris and one-sidedness, to own its own
unconscious shadow, to choose to enter into a fundamentally new relationship of mutuality with the feminine in all its forms. The feminine then becomes not
that which must be controlled, denied and exploited,
but rather fully acknowledged, respected and responded to for itself. It is recognized: not as the objec-
tified "other," but rather as source, goal, and immanent presence.*[17]

During this period in history both men and women, especially those who are trying to live out the great Christian spiritual tradition, will experience impasse, personal and societal, what St. John of
the Cross referred to as "the dark night of the soul" in a strong and frequent way that cries out for meaning. As Constance Fitzgerald points
out in her essay "Impasse and Dark Night," our experience of God and
our spirituality must emerge from our concrete, historical situation and
must return to that situation to feed and enliven it. There is not only
the dark night of the soul but the dark night of the world: "What if,
by chance, our time in evolution is a dark-night time—a time of crisis
and transition that must be understood if it is to be part of learning a
new vision and harmony for the human species and the planet?"

*The psychologists and the theologians, the poets and
the mystics, assure us that impasse can be the condition
for creative growth and transformation, if the experience of impasse is fully appropriated within one's
heart and flesh with consciousness and consent; if the
limitations of one's humanity and human condition
are squarely faced and the sorrow of finitude allowed
to invade the human spirit with real, existential
powerlessness; if the ego does not demand understanding in the name of control and predictibility, but is
willing to admit the mystery of its own being and surrender itself to this mystery; if the path into the un-*

known, into the uncontrolled and unpredictable mar-
gins of life, is freely taken when the path of deadly
clarity fails.[18]

Fundamentalists and other Christians, sensing that we are at the end of an era and that a radical change is called for, are tempted to think that we have arrived at the age of the apocalypse and the second coming. Most apocalyptic prophesy is tinged with the odor of pathological religious fear. The truth the fundamentalists sense is that the world, as they know and understand it, is coming to an end. I also believe that we have come to the end of an era; but this is not a time to run off to the mountains. It is a time to stay in the marketplace and reach out to your neighbor with compassion and genuine love. Then, if the rapture does come, you will be ready for it. But chances are that human history in God's providence has a long future still ahead.

Tarnas concludes his book with the statement that the restless inner development and incessantly innovative masculine ordering of reality characteristic of the Western mind has been gradually leading, in an immensely long dialectical movement, toward a reconciliation with the lost feminine unity, toward a profound and many-leveled marriage of the masculine and feminine, a triumphant and healing reunion. "Our time is struggling to bring forth something new in human history. We seem to be witnessing, suffering, the birth labor of a new reality, a new form of human existence, a 'child' that would be the fruit of this great archetypal marriage, and that would bear within itself all its antecedents in a new form."

This stupendous Western project should be seen as a
necessary and noble part of a great dialectic, and not
simply rejected as an imperialist-chauvinist plot. Not
only has this tradition achieved that fundamental dif-
ferentiation and autonomy of the human which alone
could allow the possibility of such a larger synthesis,
it has also painstakenly prepared the way for its own
self-transcendence. Moreover, this tradition possesses
resources, left behind and cut off by its own Prome-
thean advance, that we have scarcely begun to inte-

grate and that, paradoxically, only the opening to the feminine will enable us to integrate. Each perspective, masculine and feminine, is here both affirmed and transcended, recognized as part of a larger whole; for each polarity requires the other for its fulfillment. And their synthesis leads to something beyond itself: It brings an unexpected opening to a larger reality that cannot be grasped before it arrives, because this new reality is itself a creative act.[19]

Judy Grahn, in her book *Blood, Bread, and Roses*, holds a theory similar to that of Tarnas:

The male tradition has "the way" to sally forth in a straight line, and women (led to a great extent by feminists) have successfully followed men out of the strangling subjective matrix of the past. But men's undeviating path has also led us away from old truths and over a cliff, without "the way back." It is the women's tradition that holds the memory of the way back.

We need all the tools of humankind: arrow and loom, hierarchy and consensus, competition and cooperation, tenderness and ferocity, leisure and discipline. Men and women are not in deadly opposition. They are dancing the steps that give us human culture. . . . I believe the emergence of the Gay movements in the twentieth century also signals a crossing, especially with the connection of lesbianism to female centrality and "flow."[20]

The Lesbian and Homosexual Role in the Great Dialectic

Although to my astonishment Tarnas makes no mention of it, the emergence some twenty-five years ago of a positive gay identity on all levels—social, political, cultural, and spiritual—all over the world has a teleological purpose in the development of the *anima/animus mundi*. This presence of a visible gay and lesbian community, for the first time (to my knowledge) in the past three thousand years, is an integral part of this dialectic and is another aspect of the rediscovery of the feminine or, what I prefer to call the balancing of the masculine and feminine in a new synthesis in the human personality.

Clearly the dominant dialectic of the masculine archetype, with its repression of the feminine, has also included the repression of the homosexual. G. Rattray Taylor, in his book *Sex in History*, has pointed out that patriarchal cultures combine a subordinationist view of women with a strong repression of male homosexual practices; cultures based on a matriarchal principle, on the other hand, tend to combine an enhancement of the status of women with a relative tolerance for male homosexual practices.[21] The rise of the feminine dialectic in recent years gives us reason to hope that gays and lesbians will be fully accepted in the future human community. At the heart of all male homophobia is feminaphobia and repression of the feminine. Gay men are seen as a threat to patriarchy because they frequently are in touch with and act in accord with the feminine dimension of themselves. So the evolution of the feminine archetype potentially brings with it gay male liberation. And if it is true, as feminists tell us, that lesbians are persecuted most because they are women who refuse to play a subordinate role to men, then they too will experience liberation with the rise of the feminine archetype.

However, even if it were possible to achieve, merely adopting the new feminine archetype and repressing the masculine would not represent an improvement. In such a world gay men would continue to be oppressed, not because of their openess to the feminine, but because of their maleness, just as in this patriarchal culture lesbians are oppressed not primarily because of their lesbianism but because they are women. And there is the possibility that lesbians would continue to be oppressed because of their openness to the masculine.

Therefore, a better alternative is the emergence of a visible group that can live out fully both its masculine and feminine dimensions without the need to repress either. We need a group that will model the ideal goal of humanity's present evolution, people who can keep their feminine and masculine dimensions in good equilibrium and can bring forth a balanced synthesis of the two. This, I believe, is the providential role of the gay and lesbian political and spiritual groups that have come into being over the past twenty-five years, and it is an important aspect of the dialectic between the masculine and feminine archetypes that Tarnas has missed. Every dialectical movement toward a higher synthesis, if it is to succeed, must carry the seed of its resolution within itself.

We who are lesbian or gay must have a vision and be clear about what special gifts we bring to this moment in history. Feminists who insist that lesbians should devote all their energies to women's liberation, and not to gay liberation, are shortsighted, for they fail to understand, or consciously reject, the concept of the dialectic. Instead of a "both/and" understanding of the relation of the masculine archetype to the feminine, they adopt an "either/or" understanding, substituting the development of the feminine archetype and the repression of the masculine.

For example some feminist theologians believe it is necessary to drop a belief in Christ and Christianity because Christ is biologically male. Christianity is seen as hopelessly wedded to patriarchy, male privilege, and the repression of the feminine. And of course every troglodytic pronouncement from the Vatican against the feminist movement (against the ordination of women, for example) seems to prove them right. Consequently, they advise lesbians to drop out of gay spiritual organizations such as Dignity, Integrity, or MCC and to devote themselves exclusively to the women's liberation movement.

I am convinced that Jesus Christ's message of equality and love has been contaminated by the institutions of patriarchy, by male privilege, and by the repression of the feminine and homophobia. The time has come to cleanse ourselves and throw off these aberrations. Gay spiritual groups, I believe, are leading the way for the whole Church in bringing about this transformation.

Clearly, after three thousand years of repression, the feminist movement, still in its adolescence, must of necessity contain a rejection of the masculine archetype in order to purify and grasp the feminine in all its richness. We are at the moment when the feminine archetype's antithetical moment in the dialectic is in ascendence. This is the time for the feminine to assert its equality and dignity, and to achieve its separation from and independence of the masculine.

However, I believe that both of us, gay men and lesbian women together, have a role to play in human history, a role that would be seriously jeopardized, if we should begin to conform to an "either/or" understanding of masculine and feminine archetypes. Recently I heard a lesbian theologian, Mary Hunt, speak about the traditional Christian belief in resurrection and immortality. She agreed with Rosemary Radford Ruether that in feminine consciousness there is no need for individual immortality. Women can be satisfied with the idea that at death they will become symbiotic with the great feminine matrix in the hope that, although their ego identity is lost, new life will rise from that matrix.[22]

I believe that there is a partial truth in this position. Because of their participation in the process of birth, many women stay closer to nature and seem more at ease with the natural processes of birth, maturing, and death. If they have children, they can be more inclined to find their immortality in their offspring, rather than in their own achievements. Many of us who are male do have something to learn about accepting life processes with peace and equanimity from our sisters. But many of us, especially those without children or the possibility of children, are especially open to this message in scripture:

> *"No eunuch should say,*
> *'Look, I am a dried-up tree.'*
> *For Yahweh says this:*
> *'To the eunuchs*
> *who observe my Sabbaths*
> *and choose to do my good pleasure*
> *and cling to my covenant,*
> *I shall give them in my house*
> *and within my walls*
> *a monument and a name*
> *better than sons and daughters;*
> *I shall give them an everlasting name*
> *that will never be effaced."* (Isaiah 56:3–5)

I disagree with Mary Hunt's belief that this masculine desire for personal immortality is pathological. On the contrary, I believe men and women's desire to escape the limits of death and aspire to personal immortality is healthy. This desire falls into that category Blondel explored of human needs that are necessary for human fulfillment and impossible by human means alone.[23] Consequently, this desire for immortality opens us up to our need for the power and grace of the divine.

Winning for us this divine gift of personal immortality was the Promethean task undertaken by Jesus Christ. Perhaps this task does represent a desire present in a more pronounced way in the masculine archetype, and perhaps it can be opposed to the feminine archetypal drive to seek merger into the undifferentiated. But this difference could be one reason why the masculine dialectic had to come first. We had to achieve the ultimate levels of freedom and autonomy of the masculine archetype in order to be able to relate to God, not through symbiosis into the divine matrix, but in a free relationship of love. In the words of Pierre Teilhard de Chardin, "Must I again repeat the truth, of universal application, that, if it be properly ordered, union does not confound but differentiates!"[24]

However, that desire for personal immortality is certainly not exclusively confined to men. Every human being who has had the experience of deep personal love can find that desire in his or her own heart. Every love song ever written speaks about being "eternally" yours. We are all called into a personal relationship of love with the divine, and death cannot destroy that personal relationship. On the contrary our individual personal identity will continue beyond death for all eternity. This triumph over death is a special gift from God, which lies totally beyond our human powers. At the same time this gift responds to a profoundly felt need in the human heart.

Let me illustrate what the role of the gay community is in this dialectic with a very contemporary instance of a momentary failure of that dialectic and a reversion to the exclusively masculine archetype. During the intense debate over lifting the ban on gays in the military in 1993, I was struck by the many similarities between this debate and the debate that went on in Germany in the late twenties concerning the sodomy laws. As I described in my book *The Church and the Homosexual*, Hitler's Nazi party was well aware of the association between nonviolence and male homosexuality.[25] In the late 1920s there was a strong gay rights movement in Germany. That movement succeeded in 1928 in persuading the German government to send letters to all of Germany's political parties asking for their position on the reform of paragraph 175 of the German criminal code, a sodomy statute. The Nazi party reply was as follows:

> Munich 14 May 1928
>
> Community before Individual!
> *It is not necessary that you and I live, but it is nec-*
> *essary that the German people live. And they can only*
> *live if they can fight, for life means fighting, and they*
> *can only fight if they maintain their masculinity.*
> *They can only maintain their masculinity if they ex-*
> *ercise discipline, especially in matters of love. . . .*
> *Anyone who even thinks of homosexual love is our en-*
> *emy. We reject anything that emasculates our people*
> *and makes them a plaything of our enemies, for we*
> *know that life is a fight, and it is madness to think*
> *that men will ever embrace fraternally. Natural his-*
> *tory teaches us the opposite. Might makes right. And*
> *the stronger will always win over the weak. Let us see*
> *that we once again become the stronger.*[26]

The Nazi party's reply begins with an "either/or" proposi-tion, either the individual or the collective. Their fascist choice of the collective over the individual, surprisingly enough, represents a rejec-tion of the Promethean male archetype in favor of the feminine. The political philosophy that lay behind that judgment was a despair of building a democratic community based on the free loving commitment of individual citizens. Again we are dealing here with a half truth: the individual's rights must always be in balance in relation to the common good. As one wit put it, the rights of my fist end at the tip of your nose.

What the Nazi party wanted to gain was a total collapse of all individual rights into the collective need of the people, as they in-terpreted that need. The essential Christian message concerning the value of the individual is that each of us has a unique, unmediated re-lationship to the divine: "In truth I tell you, in so far as you neglected to do this to one of the least of these, you neglected to do it to me" (Matt. 5:45). Every one of us, then, has a value that is greater than the species or "the people." "It is better," the Sanhedrin judged, "for one man to die for the people" (John 18:14). There is a deep lesson here, that we can never legitimately subordinate the intrinsic value of any individual to the collective.

While listening to the debate over gays in the military, I heard over and over again the same message as sent by the Nazis. The super macho aggressive male self has to be maintained for the sake of the state. The Nazi debate was more honest; the issue was not sexual, the issue was love. A deep human love between members of the same sex, this was their enemy. "It is madness to think that men will ever embrace fraternally."

In 1936, Heinrich Himmler issued a decree which read: "Just as we today have gone back to the ancient German view on the question of marriages mixing different races, so too in our judgment of homosexuality—a symptom of degeneracy that could destroy our race—we must return to the guiding Nordic principle, extermination of degenerates." Orders were given that all homosexuals had to wear pink triangles in public. In 1937, the SS newspaper *Das Schwarze Korps* estimated that there were two million homosexuals in Germany and called for their extermination. Himmler gave orders that all known homosexuals were to be sent to level three concentration camps—that is death camps. As far as we know some two hundred thousand gays were worked to death.[27]

However, the injustice and the indignity did not end with the fall of the Nazi regime. After the war all other survivors of the concentration camps were treated generously in the matter of reparations. Homosexuals, however, were told that they were ineligible for compensation, since they were technically "criminals" under German law. The survivors could not even publicly protest, since they had to keep their homosexual identity secret for fear of further discrimination.

This fight over the armed forces policy has deep political and social ramifications. I do not want to feed gay paranoia by making us feel that we are as vulnerable today as we were at the time of the Nazis in 1928. The feminist liberation movement has begun the process of the dialectic, and gays are in a new, much more advanced place now in gay liberation than we were in 1928. In fact, our enemies are more frightened than we. I see the enormous antigay campaign going on today, fomented by the religious right, as clear evidence that they are fearful that they are losing the battle. And with good reason. A whole world is disappearing and it necessarily has to disappear. We must be ready, however, for moments of backlash. We must have a vision of where our movement of gay liberation is going and of what we can do both for ourselves and for the rest of humanity, our straight brothers and sisters, for we are involved in a process of liberating all human beings to the fullness of human life. This is the work of the Holy Spirit who is fundamentally at work in gay liberation and in the development of our gay spirituality, which is based first of all on equal love, the love of equals for each other, that brothers can embrace fraternally and sisters can embrace in a sisterly way.

What are these special gifts, then, that the gay and lesbian spiritual community will bring to that evolutionary process, the great dialectic between the masculine and the feminine? Tarnas makes a very strong point that the process, if it is to succeed, must retain all the gains of the past three thousand years of the development of the masculine, especially the autonomous and free individual self.

In *The Archetypes and the Collective Unconscious* Carl Jung discusses some positive aspects of male homosexuality that he had become aware of in the course of his clinical work: "This [homosexuality] gives him a great capacity for friendship, which often creates ties of astonishing tenderness between men, and may even rescue friendship between the sexes of its present limbo of the impossible."[28] Our first task, then, is to witness to deep bonds of love that exist between gay men and between lesbians and to deep bonds of loving friendship between gay men and their lesbian sisters. We must model a kind of love based on equality and respect for each other as equal subjects and no longer based on dominance and submission. Since I do not speak from within a lesbian perspective, I must leave the corresponding observations to my lesbian sisters. Mary Hunt's book, *Fierce Tenderness*, makes the point that women, once they overcome any feelings of inferiority or inadequacy as women, can make an extraordinary contribution toward building human communities based on ties of friendship rooted in equality.[29] Just imagine the strength with which new communities built on such bonds of friendship and equality might begin to remedy so many of the desperate problems we face today. Problems spawned by poverty, unemployment, racism, alcohol and drug abuse, depression, the break up of families, crime would not go untended in such communities.

As I reported in *The Church and the Homosexual*, Pierre-Claude Nappey many years ago posed what I believe is the essential question for understanding homosexuality. The fruitful question is not from whence do homosexuals come, but where are they going—or, better, for what purpose do they exist? "The question is not whether homosexuality is excusable owing to the particular circumstances of the individual concerned, but whether it is an integral part of the much vaster behavioral pattern of the collectivity and whether it contributes in some way to its proper functioning."[30]

The particular importance of that question lies in the fact that human sexual activity participates in the radical freedom of the person. Whatever participates in human freedom can only be understood adequately in terms of a teleological goal or purpose. Consequently, it is only by posing the question *why*, for what purpose, that we can hope to arrive at an adequate understanding of the human phenomenon of gay and lesbian orientation. For only by finding the answer to the teleological question can we detect in what sense homosexuality can be part of the great dialectic between the masculine and feminine archetypes being worked out in history under the guidance of the Holy Spirit. As Nappey observed: "Homosexuality must be seen . . . as corresponding to a definite finality. My own feeling is that not only is it possible for homosexuality to be of equal value with heterosexuality in individual cases, but that it has over-all significance and a special role to play in the general economy of human relations, a role that is probably irreplaceable."[31]

I believe no more urgent task faces gay liberation than determining that finality. For on its discovery depends both the ability of homosexuals and lesbians to fully accept themselves with true self-love and understanding and the ability of heterosexual society to accept a homosexual minority, not just as objects of pity and tolerance at best, but as their equals, capable of collaborating in the mutual task of building a more humane society.

What, then is the collective role of the homosexual minority in human society? And under what circumstances can that potential contribution become a reality? We have a clue to that role if we consider for a moment the frequently dehumanizing and depersonalizing role that prevailing gender-identity images play in our culture. We can summarize the objectionable stereotypes as follows: Men in our society are supposed to be strong, tough, assertive, objective, courageous, logical, constructive, independent, unsentimental, unemotional, aggressive, competitive, diligent, disciplined, level-headed, controlled, practical, promiscuous, and persuasive. Women, in turn, are supposed to be weak, passive, irrational, emotional, empty-headed, unassertive, subjective, illogical, dependent, fitful, devoted, self-effacing, impractical, artistic, and receptive.

Commenting on these stereotypes, Dr. Elinor Yaknes observed that gender identity is "the result of programming. Aside from the different physiology and anatomy . . . I cannot think of any characteristic that is uniquely the property of either sex."[32]

If we assume that these heterosexual gender identity images constitute the total mature content of the human personality, serious consequences follow. They result in a tendency to see the human individual, whether male or female, as essentially partial and incomplete. No human person is seen as complete in him or herself, but only as essentially dependent on the opposite sex for his or her completion. The insights that have come from the women's liberation movement have made us aware of the depersonalized and unequal status of women in our culture. And since men achieve their identity in part usually from their relationship to women, they in turn also suffer a depersonalized and partialized self-image.

One of the consequences of identifying with the heterosexual identity images proferred by our society is that the only type of heterosexual relationship that remains possible is a type of master-slave relationship, wherein the male seeks to dominate the female and the female seeks to be dominated. This kind of relationship leads to enormous amounts of repressed anger. And since anger is the primary anti-aphrodisiac, most heterosexual relationships in American culture cease being sexually fulfilling after a short period.

It is precisely this understanding of direct personal relationships as based on inequality of the sexes that led the young Hegel to despair of solving the problem of human unity on the personal level of interpersonal love. He was led to seek the political solution for true community in the unifying collective concept of "citizen." For he felt that it was only by taking your identity from the state and identifying with the depersonalized concept of citizen that humans felt equal to each other. This formed the basis of the Nazi concept of the subordination of all individuals to the state. Marx for similar reasons turned to class identity, "member of the proletariat," to escape the same dilemma.

Richard Mohr, in his book *Gay Ideas*, suggests that "male homoerotic relations, if institutionalized in social ritual, provide *the* most distinctive symbol for democratic values and *one* of their distinctive causes. They will help stabilize the always teetering basic structures of democracy, by serving as a model for the idea of equality.

> *The Christian metaphysical myth of the immortal individual soul with responsibility for its own destiny has done more to advance the cause of liberty and to undermine the specific thou shalt nots of Christianity itself (and of illiberal governments) than have all the splendid philosophical arguments of John Stuart Mill's* On Liberty. *In parallel, I suggest that a metaphysical myth of male homoeroticism might have a similar benefit for the more elusive concept of equality, clarifying it and causing it to become embedded in social practice more thoroughly than it could ever be through argument and reason.*[33]

Democracy, Mohr argues, will be grounded only when male homosexuality is not just tolerated, as something begrudgingly given rights, and not just accepted, as something viewed as an indifferently different life-style, and not just prized, as one admirable thing among many. Democracy will be firmly grounded only when male homosexuality is seen and treated in social ritual as a fundamental social model, when male homosexuality is, as it is in some cultures, treated as a priesthood. Here again we are dealing with a fundamental contribution of homosexuals to the political future of humanity. My lesbian friends assure me that they think Mohr's argument is equally, if not more, applicable to lesbians as well, since lesbians see themselves as men's equals and as women have always tended to deal with each other as equals.

On the theological level, true Christian love, even married

love, can exist only between persons who see themselves as somehow total and equal to each other as persons. Christian love must be love out of fullness and not out of need. It is not only the complementariness of the other sex that attracts, as Nappey observes, but "also the fact that while I sense that complementarity I can at the same time sense that here is a being who is whole and entire in himself [or herself] and . . . worthy of standing beside me and entering my life as an equal."[34] The gender stereotypes mentioned above negate any possibility of such a personal relationship for any heterosexual who takes them seriously.

Psychoanalysts maintain that all humans are basically bisexual at birth, and the normal process of becoming heterosexual involves a homosexual stage in which the child learns to identify with the parent of the same sex. This homosexual stage in the development of human sexuality has a narcissistic function. It is precisely this element of narcissism to which many moralists turn to buttress their moral condemnation of homosexuality, interpreting it in moral terms of selfishness. J. Edgar Brun, for example, makes this statement: "We may not be able to regard true inversion as a willful betrayal of the ordained social order, but the driving force of narcissism which is inevitably present in it feeds a selfishness that can always destroy the dignity of human nature."[35]

There is in this thinking a false transition from psychological narcissism to moral selfishness. Homosexual love, seen as an interpersonal relationship, can be just as selfless and other centered as heterosexual love. In fact, since it escapes the debilitating effects of the heterosexual identity images, it has a better chance to form the basis of genuinely unselfish interpersonal love.

The narcissistic function of the homosexual stage both in men and women is viewed by most psychologists as having a positive function in human sexual development.

Thanks to that function, every individual of whatever sex can learn to love him {or her} self sufficiently in order to reach the point where he {or she} will be led to take an interest in things other than himself {or herself}. This normal and legitimate dose of narcissism, this quantum of homosexuality, is what makes it possible for one human to be attracted to another.[36]

Pierre-Claude Nappey sees here not only a question of individual psychology but of global collective psychology. He sees, as a consequence, the homosexual community as playing the role of objectifying a necessary stage in human sexual development. If the day should come when it is possible to repress all homosexual tendencies, so that the homosexual should disappear from the face of the earth, we should then face the danger of removing a creative catalyst for the progressive development of sexual relations toward a fuller and more human reality.

> *If heterosexuals honestly wish to see the perfect integration of persons and of the sexes, if they honestly hope to see the establishment of the best possible conditions for the fulfillment of individuals and of society as a whole, they will have to try to accept their own homosexuality through the acceptance of those in whom homosexuality is explicit. . . . Why shouldn't everyone be delighted that homosexuals have been entrusted* de facto *with the task and mission of attending the flame, or rather the two original flames, which, if they were to go out, would no longer serve as catalyzers of heterosexuality, thereby bringing the downfall of the entire system.*[37]

Eugene Kennedy points to the same creative role of the homosexual in relationship to the heterosexual community. He writes of the beneficial consequences of a greater acceptance of homosexuality in society, so that the process leading to our gender identity and sexual orientation will be based less in fear of nonconformity and more in a challenge to be true to the authentic self.

> *When humans can face with less fear the complex of feelings and impulses that are part of each person's sexuality, they will be able to accept and integrate their experience into a less prejudiced and more creative self-identity. That is to say, when persons can be more friendly toward what really goes on inside them, they will feel less pressure to deny or distort their experience*

of themselves; the achievement of their masculine or
feminine identity will be less the acceptance of a rig-
idly imposed social stereotype and more the attain-
ment of a multi-dimensional truth about themselves.
Greater openness to self can only increase our chance
of more successful gender identity.[38]

Traditionally the married relationship between male and female found its support and stability in social roles, customs, and laws
which rendered relatively secondary the type of direct personal relationship between the parties involved. But all these social supports are rapidly fading away, with the result that the divorce rate in the United
States has approached the 50 percent mark. Clearly, genuine personal
love uniting husband and wife as equals will be needed to sustain the
heterosexual family.

If the homosexual community were allowed to play its role
in society with full acceptance, homosexuals would cease to play their
present negative role of undermining marriage relationships into which
they have been forced by their desire to escape detection. Instead, they
could be a help in leading society to a new and better understanding of
interpersonal love between equals—rather than the role playing determined by tradition—as the foundation for the marriage relationship.

One often hears the opinion expressed that homosexuality
represents an immature form of sexual development at a narcissistic
stage, which prevents the individual from appreciating the difference of
the opposite sex. However, frequently it is the male heterosexual who,
being under the influence of socially constructed sexual identity images,
is preoccupied with the opposite sex as a "sexual object" to be dominated. The perfect example of this preoccupation is *Playboy*'s bunny image, a deliberate effort to depersonalize and reduce the members of the
opposite sex to animal status in order to escape the guilt of using and
abusing them as sexual objects. Since the heterosexual male so often sees
the other only in the generic context of sex object, he cannot relate to
the other as truly "other"—that is as person. Whereas the gay person,
to the extent that he or she has been freed from the depersonalizing effect
of these images, is more free to encounter the other person as total in
him or herself and as an equal person.

In a particularly prophetic passage Rainer Maria Rilke had this to say about the changing role of women:

> *We are only just now beginning to look upon the relation of an individual person to a second individual objectively and without prejudice, and our attempts to live such associations have no model before them. . . . The girl and the women, in their new, their own unfolding, will but in passing be imitators of masculine ways, good and bad, and repeaters of masculine professions. After the uncertainty of such transitions it will become apparent that women were only going through the profusion and the vicissitudes of those (often ridiculous) disguises in order to cleanse their own characteristic nature of the distorting influence of the other sex. . . . The humanity of women, borne its full time in suffering and humiliation, will come to light when she will have stripped off the conventions of mere femininity in the mutations of her outward status . . . some day there will be girls and women whose name will no longer signify merely an opposite to the masculine, but something in itself, something that makes one think, not of any complement or limit, but only of life and existence: the feminine human being. This advance will change the love experience, which is now full of error, will alter it from the ground up, reshape it into a relation that is meant to be of one human being to another, no longer of man to women. And this more human love (that will fulfill itself, infinitely considerate, and gentle, and kind, and clear in binding and releasing) will resemble that which we are preparing with struggle and toil, the love that consists in this, that two solitudes protect, border and salute each other.*[39]

The second attribute that Jung assigns to gay men is an aesthetic sensitivity to beauty: "He [the homosexual] may have good taste and an aesthetic sense which are fostered by the presence of a feminine streak."[40] One of the greatest revelations that God has made of herself in this world is through beauty. "Late have I loved you, O Beauty, ever ancient, ever new. Late have I loved you!" reads the famous prayer of St. Augustine. I love that name for God, Beauty, because it is genderless. I have found that gay people are, indeed, extraordinarily open to beauty. There is no doubt that homosexual men are freer to develop aesthetic values than heterosexual men. Heterosexual men living out the male stereotype cannot be open to beauty and are fearful and ashamed if they show any sensitive response to beauty. Yet one of the greatest revelations that God makes of herself is through beauty.

Gay men, then, have important roles to play in guiding humanity to a deeper appreciation of aesthetic values. Many of the great creators of art, sculpture, music, architecture, drama, all the fine arts have come from the gay community. There is an extraordinary amount of glory given to God through the creation of beauty that comes from the gay community. One of the great tragedies of the AIDS epidemic is that so many of our talented gay brothers who were enormously creative have been dying before they completed their life's work.

The third attribute that Jung assigns to gay men is: "He may be supremely gifted as a teacher because of his almost feminine insight and tact."[41] The attraction of many homosexuals to service roles, where they have been particularly successful, has gone relatively unnoticed by our culture, since in the past they were compelled to remain hidden in the closet. The gift of compassion is one of the gifts many gay men receive almost simultaneously with their gayness. This is something that we gay men have to be grateful for. Everywhere I go, if I find a tactful, insightful, sensitive man engaged in compassionate human service, working with the sick, the retarded, the blind, the disabled, or children, more often than not, he is gay. This is also true of the ministry; more often than not when I have come across a man who is doing wonderful ministry, I can be pretty sure that he is gay.

Another positive effect that homosexuality can have on men, according to Jung, is their "feeling for history" and their resultant tendency "to be conservative in the best sense and cherish the values of the past."[42] Since the majority of traditional values have their basis in the heterosexual family structure, Jung's observation seems rather paradoxical; in fact, to the radical right, the homosexual appears as a threat to the family structure and, as a consequence, a threat to all those values traditionally associated with it. However, most of those traditional values represent customs, mores, and taboos imposed from without to which the majority give uncritical conformity. Forced because of their homosexual condition to live for the most part outside these structures, self-accepting gay people are thrown back on themselves and their own experience in order to reestablish those values which merit their acceptance. Almost in direct proportion as they are cut off from traditional patterns, they must seek out and recreate the real values which these patterns were meant to convey and must preserve them by their personal commitment.

Jung's final, surprising observation concerning the positive aspects of male homosexuality has to do with the religious and spiritual development of humanity. "He [the gay person] is endowed with a wealth of religious feelings which help him bring the *ecclesia spiritualis* into reality, and a spiritual receptivity which makes him responsive to revelation."[43]

In 1977, I was called in by the board of ministry of the United Church of Christ to consult on the question of ordaining the first out-of-the-closet gay minister, Bill Johnson. At that time I read this quotation from Jung to them and suggested that if Jung's observation were true, and I had long been certain that it is true, they should not debate the question: Shall we ordain a gay man? Rather, they should debate the issue: Shall we ordain a heterosexual?

The spiritual process of accepting our exile status in this world and giving up the myth that we can find our meaning exclusively in this world can result in great spiritual freedom. That freedom can help us to live fearlessly and authentically in this world. By deepening our spiritual lives, we can turn what many see as the curse of gayness or the curse of being a social outcast into spiritual gold. Matthew Kelty, a Trappist monk, speaks of this aspect of gayness in his book *Flute Solo: Reflections of a Trappist Hermit*:

> *Sometimes I wish I were more like others. I am aware*
> *of a difference; some insight into things, some capacity*

for the poetic and the spiritual which, if not excep-
tional—and it is not—is still strong enough to set me
off from others. Nor do I hesitate to say that this has
some relationship to homosexuality. For though I have
never practiced it, I am well aware of an orientation
that is certainly as much in that direction as the other;
further, that given the knowledge, the opportunity, the
circumstances, I could easily as not have gone in that
direction. But people of my kind seem often so placed,
the reason, as I have worked it out, that they are more
closely related to the "anima" than is usual. . . .
What such people yearn for is solace in their solitude
and an understanding of their fate, their des-
tiny. . . . The man with a strong anima will always
experience some inadequacy until he comes to terms
with his inner spirit and establishes communion—no
small achievement. Until then he cannot act truly as
a complete person, since he is not one. He will then be
unable to relate in depth to others. The unhappy ex-
perience of many is that they are unable to relate to
others, not aware that their problem is a lack of com-
munion with themselves. The blind comfort the blind,
but they cannot open each other's eyes. . . . Perhaps a
healthy culture would enable those so gifted by God or
nature {i.e., homosexuals} to realize their call and
respond to it in fruitful ways.[44]

What then must we gay people do to transform our curse of
difference into a blessing? If we find time each day to spend in God's
presence in prayer, we will develop a living, affectionate, personal relationship with God. We will then be able to recognize all the broken
events in our lives—the losses, the pain, and the grief—as connected
with and given meaning by the great events of God's redemptive work
in Jesus. If we pray daily, then God will give us the grace to be fully
prepared for death. For if we enter freely into the presence of God every
day, how easy it should be for those of us who have already mourned and

let go of the myth of belonging in this world to enter once and for all into the presence of our divine lover at the moment of death. *Maranatha!* Come, Lord Jesus, Come!

The Holy Spirit is working deeply in the history of this world to bring about the reign of God. This reign includes the establishment of justice and peace in history itself, in this world. To participate in this dialectic, we are at a critical moment when both men and women must incorporate and open themselves up to the feminine archetype in a very real synthesis with the positive accomplishments reaped from the three-thousand-year history of the development of the masculine archetype.

In his letters, Paul speaks of the Holy Spirit working in the world to help us overcome all the divisions that separate us from each other and therefore cut us off from ourselves (Gal. 3:28). The only way that I can be one with myself is to be one with all humanity without exception, no racial exceptions, no gender exceptions, no exceptions because of sexual orientation. Don't forget Jesus' name for himself was "son of man," or, as we would say today, "son of humanity." Paul mentions three great divisions that remain to be overcome through the reconciling work of the Holy Spirit. The first is the overcoming of the master-slave division, including the elimination of slavery of all kinds, the establishment of political freedom for all humans. This task is still going on.

The second division Paul mentions is the division between Jew and Greek; by that he meant all divisions based on race, nationality, ethnicity, and religion. The Holy Spirit will work in the world to undo all these divisions so that we will understand ourselves as brothers or sisters of every human being that exists and not feel any separation because of racial, religious, or ethnic difference.

The final division that must be overcome is the division between male and female. We must become equals and become one with our sisters or brothers outside ourselves. And in so doing, we can become one with the feminine or the masculine in ourselves.

Overcoming those divisions is a very slow historical process that has been going on over centuries. But today, I believe, the gay spiritual movement has emerged out of the heart of the world to play a decisive role in overcoming this final division. Again, let us remember that Scripture says that the stone that was rejected will become the cornerstone. The gay spiritual communities are being called by God to play this "cornerstone" role. The only way, however, that gays can play that role is to overcome their fears and have the courage to come out of the closet. Gays must model in a very public way their ability to balance the masculine and feminine dimensions within themselves, their ability to put together genuine gay human love for each other with a deep spiritual life, and their deep awareness of the presence of the Holy Spirit in their life. They must become, therefore, "candles on the hilltop" for everyone to see.

The cornerstone role is a real challenge. But you can be certain that if you are gay or lesbian the Holy Spirit is calling you to take some steps in that direction, to be more open about your gayness, to be more open about the depth of your spiritual life. We must seek God's grace because a cornerstone, after all, is a small, if essential, part of a building, the entirety of which is the work of the Holy Spirit. The Spirit waits on our freedom to invite her in to make use of our gifts and talents in bringing about the reign of God, a reign of justice and peace, a reign where God's glory is achieved through the fullness of life that all humans share, gay and straight alike.

APPENDIX 1

MAURICE BLONDEL: *The* PHILOSOPHER *of* FREEDOM

I will never forget the joy and excitement I felt the first time I read the philosophical thought of Maurice Blondel. I was a student of theology at Woodstock College, a Jesuit Seminary in Maryland. I hungered for a philosophical framework which I could use to integrate my religious faith with the deep insights coming from the human sciences, especially psychology. At the same time, I was intensely aware of the inadequacies of traditional Thomistic philosophy to provide that framework. I found in Blondel a kindred spirit whose philosophical thought remains an original and profound response to the problems and the needs of our time.

Blondel defined philosophy as "life itself insofar as it attempts to achieve a clear reflexive consciousness of itself."[1] I appreciated the holistic tone of that definition; philosophy has as its object the whole of human life and not just language or thought in abstraction from life. In his first great work, *L'Action: Essai d'une Critique de la Vie et d'une Science de la Pratique*, published in 1893, Blondel took his central insight from a verse in Scripture, "but whoever does the truth comes out into the

195

light" (John 3:21). Blondel saw human life as a continual dialectic between thought and action. He liked to compare the human intellect to the headlights of a car. Those headlights can illuminate our way only as far as the next curve in the road. The car must move forward to that curve before the headlights can illuminate what lies around that curve. In a similar way, each of us must act according to our understanding in order to arrive at the fullness of "light" or wisdom. There is a kind of subjective experiential knowing that comes from human choice and action and cannot be achieved in any other way.[2]

This insight lies at the heart of all modern efforts of human liberation. For example, women derive a unique kind of knowledge of themselves from their subjective experience of themselves as women. Lesbians and gays have a subjective source of knowledge of what it means to be gay or lesbian that comes from their immediate experience of themselves in their lives and actions and which is not obtainable in any other way. The poor have a unique knowledge that comes from their experience of poverty. The only way we who do not share that subjective experience can obtain that knowledge is by listening carefully and respectfully to those who do have that subjective experience and can articulate its meaning.

The question Blondel proposed to explore is the central question: What is the meaning of human life and its common destiny? Blondel contends that humans cannot choose to cease being; we are here, like it or not, for eternity.

> *Yes or no, has life a meaning and do humans have a destiny? I act without knowing what action is, without having wished to live. . . . This appearance of being that is at work in me, these actions fleeting as a shadow, I understand that they carry within them the weight of an eternal responsibility, and even at the cost of blood I cannot purchase nothingness, because for me it can no longer be. I find myself condemned to life, condemned to death, condemned to eternity. Why and by what right, since I have neither known nor willed it.*[3]

Having posed the question of human destiny, Blondel makes the point that freedom is the very essence of the human subject and the essential condition of possibility for human existence. There can be no human destiny, unless that destiny can be achieved through human freedom. Blondel makes the passionate assertion that each of us must be able to choose life, choose death, choose eternity, otherwise the very existence of the human is an illusion. "There is no being where there is only constraint. If I am not that which I will to be, I am not. At the very core of my being there is a will and a love of being or there is nothing. If human freedom is real, it is necessary that one have at present or at least in the future a knowledge and a will sufficient never to suffer any tyranny whatsoever."[4]

Blondel's understanding of human freedom differed radically from the classical understanding of scholastic realism. The scholastics believed that humans were substantially determined by their essence and only free on the superficial level of actions. Blondel believed that for a human to be is to act, and in acting, to freely mold his or her own reality. Humans are not totally nor authentically human unless in the depth of their being and action they seize themselves as a free source, action itself, a constant self-positing. Human freedom is understood as the radical self-positing of our own reality. We must exist at every moment as a consequence of our freedom. If in the depths of our own subjective being we meet with any determinism whatsoever—biological, psychological, social, or even a determinism springing from the divine will, a determinism which lies radically outside the sphere of our free ability to determine ourselves—then we would be forced to accept the conclusion that the existence of the individual human person as such is an illusion.

This insight into the radical nature of human freedom led Blondel to accept the principle of immanence as the fundamental methodological principle governing his philosophy. He formulated that principle in these words, "Nothing can impose itself on a human, nothing can demand the assent of her or his intellect or the consent of his or her will which does not find its source from within ourselves." I dealt with the principle of immanence in chapter 10 as one of the ways to resolve the differences of masculine and feminine understandings of God in twelve-step spirituality. "That necessity which appears to me as a tyrannous constraint, that obligation which at first appears despotic, in the last analysis, it is necessary that I understand it as manifesting and activating the most profound reality of my own will; otherwise it will be my destruction."[5]

Anything that presents itself from without as essential to the achievement of human destiny and happiness must correspond to a need in the dynamic of the human will or, on the psychological level, to a profoundly felt desire in the depths of the human psyche. Blondel did not hesitate to apply this methodological principle of immanence to any manifestation of the divine will. Although the divine will must manifest itself as in some way distinct from our finite will, yet that revelation, if it is not to destroy our freedom and integrity, must be made in some way from within our consciousness of self and prove capable of being assimilated into our free self-positing.

The entire movement of modern philosophy has been a continual movement toward a deeper understanding of the role the subject as such plays in human understanding and willing. This movement has led to the conclusion that there is only one possible method to attain the existing subject as such in its unique freedom in a legitimate philosophical manner; we must renounce all attempts to make the singular existing subject into an objective content of knowledge, and be content to seize it in our immediate experiential awareness of self in the deployment of our free activity.

All too often we are tempted to conceive of freedom and determinism as contradictories; either we humans are determined or we are free. In an attempt to resolve that dilemma, many philosophers have embraced a form of dualism which views the human as flesh and spirit, given over to total determinism in the flesh, but free only in the spirit. Such an understanding leads to a dichotomy between freedom of intention and determinism of actions.

The very concept "freedom" expresses not an absolute but a relative capacity. From what are we as humans freed and for what are we freed? Because of our self-consciousness and power of reflection, we humans have the negative power to suspend the automatic operation of all determinisms, whether they be biological, psychological, or social. We also have the positive power to project ideal goals, which represent not that which is, meaning that which is given from the past, but also that which ought to be. Since what ought to be does not yet exist, it cannot be understood as exercising a mechanistic style of determinism on the human action it influences. Rather than understanding human freedom as a contradiction of determinism, that freedom can be better understood as a new form of determinism, the substitution of the pull of ideals from ahead for the purely compulsive and unconscious *vis a tergo*, a push from the rear.

Human freedom, then, represents our power to transcend what is factually given from the past, precisely by projecting what ought to be as an ideal goal in the future. The possibility of incorporating those transcendental ideals into our actions by a free choice leads to an awareness of that action as a properly free moral action, and of self as a free moral agent. Humans are, thus, freed from all predeterminism: " . . . the will is led to place the center of its equilibrium beyond all factual realities, to live as it were on itself, to search in itself alone the purely formal reasons of its acts."[6]

The creative power of the moral act is to be found in the power of the will to synthesize a given set of ideals into the factual reality of its activity by free choice. Humans on the moral level are characterized by self-development. We perceive every choice as a choice between authentic and inauthentic humanity. We see our lives as having a meaning only we can give it through our free choice.

The Religious Dimension of Blondel's Dialectic of Will

Blondel understood the moral development of human life as a dialectic we experience between will-willing and will-willed, where will-willing refers to the capacity or potentiality of the will for perfect fulfillment and the will-willed represents that part of that potentiality that each of us has actualized through our free choices. A key concept for Blondel is the concept of "privation." Privation is a third category between pure actuality and nothingness; it is defined as "the absence of that which ought to be."[7] Like the missing piece in a jigsaw puzzle, one can define what is missing. What is missing, then, has a definable negative presence in the will. What is privative in life can be experienced on the psychological level as absence and longing. It is precisely what is experienced as privative in human life that we project out as an ideal goal of our striving. I dealt with Blondel's concept of privation in chapter 6. Blondel maintained that " . . . in the very activity itself of our will is revealed the end to which it necessarily tends and the series of means which it must use. There is a necessary logic of freedom. Human actions can be illogical; they can never be alogical. Either one conforms freely to the law which one carries within oneself, or one opposes it freely, one can never escape it."[8]

This understanding of the dialectic of will led Blondel to a new understanding of truth. Traditionally within objective realism truth was defined as the conformity of our ideas with objective reality. Blondel understood the truth of free human action as the conformity of our free choices with the necessary dynamic of the human will. Accepting the Kantian critique of objective realism, that there is never any way to be sure that the ideas in our mind correspond exactly to objective reality, Blondel replied:

> As long as we see the X to be discovered in the relation of thought and object . . . there is no solution and no real progress is conceivable. But it is altogether different once the unknown is within us, in ourselves. Once, in a word, the truth to be conquered is not an external abstraction, but an internal concrete reality. For if the X of objective thought is inaccessible and indeterminable, the X of our own proper equation with ourselves can be obtained and determined step by step. . . . The solution is already within us, already provisionally determined by each of our moments which could be our last.[9]

To be true means to become that which one ought to be. The search for truth on the reflective level becomes, then, a search for what one must will to become authentically one with all the potentiality in the self. On the psychological level this becomes a search for the mature authentic self. Blondel agreed with Aristotle's definition of happiness as "using all our potentialities at a certain degree of excellence."

Final Option

Blondel began his study of human freedom with the famous quote: "I find myself condemned to life, condemned to death, condemned to eternity. If my freedom does not give final meaning to my life, I am not; as a human person I have no meaning or identity. I must be free to choose life, to choose death, to choose eternity, or I am nothing."[10] Consequently, my freedom, if it is real and not an illusion, must be able to enter into the very process of dying.

The option for or against transcendence reveals itself in Blondel's understanding of the dialectic of action as the final necessary condition of human freedom.[11] Every free human agent is necessarily faced with the decision to accept or refuse the present of the transcendent within his or her will. The two extreme and contradictory responses to that interior appeal can be either total openness, *disponibilité* without condition, or a will to self-sufficiency, a pretension to dispose of oneself as master of one's own destiny, what Marcel calls *refus de l'invocation*. Blondel maintained that an option is necessarily implied implicitly in every free human commitment. Depending on the alternative, the option resolves itself in either possession or privation of self, the world and God. In other words, the human will ultimately resolves itself in the identity of truth or the real contradiction of error.

Blondel believed that this option, implicit in every human choice, necessarily becomes explicit in the process of dying. For judgment to make human sense, our moment of death must, with the help of God's grace, be a moment of free choice into which the whole history of our lives and all the free choices we have made in our lifetime enter as vector forces. We must be free to make our final choice in the presence of God. All the good, loving, unselfish choices of our life will lead us to choose to enter into union with incarnate love. All our bad, unloving, selfish choices will exert pressure on us to separate ourselves from a presence we experience as painful. And yet our final moment will be one in which we choose and decide what final meaning we will give our lives.[12] If God truly created us free, then He/She must allow us this final option. We must be able to freely choose the nature of our eternity. This is why all religious traditions have always considered the moment of death as so critical: "Pray for us now and at the moment of our death. Amen!"

The most beautiful and accurate image of final judgment that I know, one in total conformity with Blondel's understanding of "final option," occurs in C. S. Lewis's book *The Last Battle*, the seventh volume in his *Chronicles of Narnia*. In this book, Aslan, a lion who is the Christ-figure and savior of his world, stands in the doorway of his stable, the same stable in which he was born. One by one, the sun, moon, and stars are extinguished until there is only one source of light left; that which issues from the entrance to the stable. All the creatures of that world rush toward that source of light and come face to face with Aslan. Those who hated him in their lifetime and refused his rule of love are filled with loathing and dread when they see him and choose freely to run off into the darkness on his left. But those who loved him and kept his rule of love are filled with joy and run up to hug him and enter into the light on his right.

In this scene, Aslan, the God-figure, does nothing; God is what God is. It is the creatures who judge themselves according to how they choose to relate to him. Both Blondel's philosophy of freedom and Lewis's retelling of the last judgment make clear the ultimate dimension of our moral freedom: whether we put God into our lives or exclude Her/His loving presence depends completely on our own choice. We should, therefore, conceive of our death as the opportunity for a decisive and definitive act of free commitment in love, a giving ourselves once and for all into the hands of God: "Into your hands I commit my spirit" (Luke 23:46).

Don Pedro Arrupé, the General of the Society of Jesus, shortly before he lapsed into his final coma, was asked to share his understanding of death:

> *In reality, death, which is sometimes feared so much, is for me one of the most anticipated events, an event that will give meaning to my life. Death can be considered as an end to life and as a threshold to eternity; in both of these aspects I find consolation. As the end to life, it is still the end of a life that is nothing else than a path crossing a desert to approach eternity. . . . In as much as death is also the threshold of eternity, it involves the entrance into eternity that*

> *is at the same time unknown and longed for; it involves*
> *meeting the Lord and an eternal intimacy with him.*
> *What will heaven be like? It is impossible to imagine.*
> *Eternity, immortality, beatific vision, perfect happi-*
> *ness—it's all new, nothing is known. Is death, then,*
> *a leap into the void? No, of course not! It is to throw*
> *yourself into the arms of the Lord; it is to hear the*
> *invitation, unmerited, but given in all sincerity:*
> *"Well done, good and faithful servant . . . come and*
> *enter into the joy of your master (Matt. 25:21); it is*
> *to come to the end of faith and hope in order to live in*
> *eternal and infinite love (1 Cor. 2:9). I hope my death*
> *will be a "consummatum est," all is finished, the final*
> *amen of my life, and the first alleluia of my eternity.*[13]

These are obviously the words of a human who has nothing to fear in making the final option.

It took enormous courage for the young Blondel to publish his *Philosophy of Action* with its passionate defense of human freedom. The Church resented his attack on the synthesis of theology with Thomism. There was a serious threat in Rome to condemn his work. Cardinal Montini (who later became Pope Paul VI) was his defender and won for him the compromise that, if he promised never to publish anything further, his work would not be put on the index of forbidden books. As a result Blondel never published another major work in his lifetime. He became progressively blind in later life, and his subsequent work was published only after his death. He was the first of a long line of prophetic thinkers in the Roman Catholic Church who became victims of that Church's anti-intellectualism. Posthumously, Blondel's reputation as a philosopher of religion was acknowledged at the Second Vatican Council. Many of his disciples, among them Karl Rahner, Ives Congar, Henri De Lubac, and Teilhard de Chardin, were the principal theologians whose thought led to the Vatican II Council, and his name was mentioned in the debates on the council floor over sixty times.

At the same time because of his public affirmation of his religious belief, despite his brilliance and originality, Blondel was denied any teaching position in the French university system by the atheist minister of education. After several years, he was finally assigned a teaching position at the University of Aix/Marseille, the French university furthest removed from the intellectual center in Paris. This punishment was occasioned by the courageous final statement Blondel made in defense of his thesis: "However, if I can be permitted to add one word, one final word that goes beyond the proper domain of the human sciences and the competence of philosophy, that unique word which is capable, as a result of Christian revelation, to express the best part of that certitude which cannot be had unless it rises up from the intimacy of a personal action, a word which is in itself an action, then, I must pronounce it: God exists ("C'est")."[14]

APPENDIX 2

The CHURCH and the HOMOSEXUAL: ITS CONDEMNATION and MY RESPONSE

In 1977, at the time that I was ordered to silence by the Vatican on the issue of homosexuality and the *imprimi potest*, the official permission to publish from religious authorities, was ordered removed from *The Church and the Homosexual*, I asked my provincial (my religious superior) for a written account of the reasons for this action. That request was refused. As a result, there was an outcry among Church lawyers that I had been denied my right in canon law to receive a written account of the charges against me. I was never personally given that written account. But in its lieu in the summer of 1978 the Congregation for the Doctrine of the Faith, the Vatican congregation in charge of protecting faith and morals, published in *Origins*, a periodical devoted to official Roman documents, a letter concerning my book. This letter was addressed to Fr. Pedro Arrupé, the General (major superior) of the Society of Jesus, from Cardinal Ratzinger, the prefect of the Congregation. It was filled with distortions and half-truths and maligned my character. At that time, since I was ordered to silence, I let it go unanswered. But since the letter has now been republished in *Readings in Moral Theology, No.8: Dialogue about Catholic Sexual Teaching* (Paulist Press, 1993), I want to respond publicly and share my frustration and anger at the distortions and falsehoods that letter contained.[1] The letter reads as follows:

1

The congregation first intends to clarify certain points concerning the nature and publication of this book.

1. *The book*, The Church and the Homosexual, *clearly and openly advocates a moral position regarding homosexuality which is contrary to—in theory as well as in practice—the traditional and actual teaching of the church.*

In his own words, the author presents an "advocacy theology" (p. 24) for "ethically responsible homosexual relationships" (p.198 and passim*). The contents of this book are arranged to show that there is no proven moral obligation to refrain from "ethically responsible homosexual relationships" and that, therefore, both church and civil norm must accept these relationships as legitimate. . . .*

2. *The book was published with the* imprimi potest *of the Jesuit provincial superior, Father Eamon Taylor; the* imprimatur *was not requested because, according to the judgment of the canonist consulted, "permission is recommended but not prescribed," and in this case "the purpose of the recommendation has already been fulfilled through the extensive process of examination . . . and the further delays which would be entailed in requesting diocesan approval would constitute a disproportionate inconvenience to the author, the publisher. . . ."*

This point is important: What is the purpose *of the* imprimi potest *which was given? Although the* imprimatur *is strongly recommended in a case of this sort (cf. this congregation's* Decretum de Ecclesiae Pastorum vigilantia circa libros *of March 19, 1975), it is not required; the permission of the com-*

petent superior, however, is required according to the
constitutions of the Jesuit Order. The imprimi potest
given would normally indicate that the contents of the
book were judged to be sound, in accord with the
Church's teaching, and safe to follow in practice. This
is clearly not the case with Father McNeill's book.

Father McNeill explains in the Preface to his book
his understanding of the significance of the imprimi
potest:

"It is important for the reader to understand what
is implied in the granting of an ecclesiastical imprimi potest, i.e., permission to publish, by my religious superiors and what is not implied. First, the
authorities that grant the permission in no way commit themselves as agreeing or disagreeing with the content of the book. Rather, all that is implied is that
authorities have assured that the book is a prudent
work that meets the standards of scholarship for the
publication of a book on a controversial moral topic.
Secondly, the 'permission to publish' in no way implies
that the conclusions stated in this book are accepted by
the Catholic Church as part of its official teaching;
only the Pope and the bishops have the authority to
teach officially in the name of the church" (cf. pp.
221–22).

Normally, however, the imprimi potest is the superior's permission based on the censor's judgment that
the book does not contain errors or advice which would
be harmful to its readership.

For this reason, it seems important to note the explanation given by the provincial superior, Father Eamon G. Taylor, S.J., in granting the imprimi potest. His reason in departing from the customary
norms governing the granting of the imprimi potest
seems to be based on the fact that he envisions a restricted readership for the book—one for whom the
danger of scandal could be reasonably said not to ex-

ist. *Father Taylor's prepared statement on his* imprimi potest *stated:*

*"The permission to publish granted by ecclesiastical
superiors does not imply any judgment of the content
or opinions expressed in the book. It does imply that
the work has been judged competently and responsibly
written, and therefore,* suitable for presentation to
and evaluation by scholars. . . . *The ultimate
judgment upon Father McNeill's method and conclusion will come from* his peers among professional
moral theologians, and from the magisterial authority *of the church, to which Father McNeill defers" (emphasis ours).*

*In this explanation, Father Taylor appeals to
"scholars" and "peers" in the field of moral theology
as the intended readership justifying the permission to
publish.*

*On the other hand, it seems apparent to us that the
kind of scholarly and peer-group readership envisioned
by the provincial superior was not at all the audience
Father McNeill and his publishers had in mind. We
conclude this both from his stated intention in the
Preface of his book, and from the speeches and lectures
he has given in city after city to promote the book's sale
and its thesis on homosexuality. The intention of Father McNeill is clear; he says:*

"The imprimi potest *was important to me, first
of all, because it is my hope that this book will help
foster an all-out discussion of the Church's moral understanding and pastoral practice concerning the homosexual. Secondly, I* particularly want to reach,
and open up new, hopeful possibilities for, all
those Catholic homosexuals *who are struggling to
put together their dual identities as Catholics and as
homosexuals. Therefore, it was important to me that
the book should be accepted into the* mainstream of

Catholic debate *and reflection (p. 221, emphasis ours)."*

Father McNeill further indicated his intention of giving the widest possible publicity to his theological and pastoral opinions, when he comments on the developments leading up to the publication in this way:

"Almost simultaneously with the offer of publication, I received a notice from my Jesuit superiors that Father General Pedro Arrupé, S.J., had written from Rome ordering me not to publish anything in the popular press and not to address homosexual groups. . . . I was particularly upset by this prohibition, first because the implication of the letter that the moral debate could be carried on outside the notice of the public media and exclusively on a peer-group level *seemed to me totally impracticable; and secondly because I was convinced that it was* only through open discussion, *with the Catholic homosexual community participating as an equal partner, that any real advance could be made in the Church's moral understanding of homosexuality and consequent pastoral practice (p. 219, emphasis ours).*

Father McNeill indicates he took the attitude of some of the scholars on the commission which the Jesuit authorities set up to judge his work as encouragement to pursue a course of publicizing his ideas among the entire Catholic and secular community, rather than aim for the community of scholarship: " . . . a majority of the commission reported that they found the manuscript a serious and scholarly work worthy of publication. Several felt strongly that there should be a public debate *on all the issues involved and that my manuscript would be an important contribution to that debate" (p. 220).*

It seems clear that Father Taylor's stated purpose

*and the purpose and course of action of Father
McNeill do not coincide. Therefore, even apart from
a judgment about the wisdom of granting the imprimi potest in the first place, it seems altogether
reasonable and necessary to withdraw it now.*

*3. We find it extraordinary that a book so clearly
contradicting the moral teaching of the church would
be published a few days after the publication of* Persona humana, *a document of this congregation treat-
ing in part of the same question; no reasonable person
could imagine that time for serious study and evaluation had been given to the declaration of the authentic
magisterium of the church in this case. Such an action
cannot but indicate the gravest sort of disregard for
the mature study of and loyal support for the teachings
of the church expected of her sons, especially those who
have positions of responsibility through the reception of
holy orders. The following extracts from the article in*
Time *magazine (Sept. 20, 1976) is an example of
how well this situation is understood by society at
large:*

*"When the Congregation for the Doctrine of the
Faith issued its 5,000-word statement on homosexuality, premarital sex, and masturbation, it was responding in part to complaints that the church was not
providing sufficient guidelines for sexual behavior and
attitudes. Days later, Father John McNeill, a Jesuit
priest and former teacher of moral theology at the now
defunct Woodstock College and at Fordham University, won the designation* imprimi potest *(it can be
printed) for a book strongly attacking the church's
view on homosexuality."*

*4. Finally, we think it important to clarify the is-
sue regarding the scandal caused by this book. The
scandal comes from the content of the book itself—
ideas and suggested pastoral practice clearly at vari-
ance with the teaching and practice of the church; from*

the circumstances of publication—the imprimi potest *gives the aura of ecclesiastical approval, and the
publication of the book within days after* Persona humana *gravely damages the respectful attitude toward
the teaching of the authentic magisterium of the church
in the public view; and from the publicity and promotion given to the book and its ideas by Father
McNeill himself through his tour of public lectures
and press conferences.*

*One measure of the seriousness of this scandal is the
extraordinary step taken by the president of the episcopal conference in the United States. Archbishop Joseph Bernardin of Cincinnati, on the occasion of the
publicity given to Father McNeill's scheduled appearance in his archdiocese:*

*"This weekend Father John McNeill, S.J., will
be in the city to speak about his new book,* The
Church and the Homosexual. *Because his visit has
already been given public notice and because his lecture
will also be given publicity, I wish to restate the
church's position regarding homosexuality so there will
be no confusion in the minds of people . . . No one can
take it upon himself to alter this clear teaching. While
it is legitimate for theologians to explore this moral
question like any other, it is a disservice to challenge
this teaching publicly in such a way as to give the
impression that some radical change has taken place or
is about to take place."*

*Such appearances by Father McNeill in various
cities throughout the United States continue.to be a
source of scandal, both in the false hopes given to
Catholic homosexuals and in the confusion caused in
the community at large. These public appearances
clearly indicate that the purpose originally stated for
granting the* imprimi potest *by Father Taylor—
"its presentation to and evaluation by scholars"—has
long been set aside.*

II

After the explicit clarification of the facts of the case by the above considerations, we are best able to address the second point: What steps or actions would be suitable to avoid further scandal? It seems to us that the following actions should be taken at a minimum:

1. Father Taylor should be required to withdraw the imprimi potest, *so that it would not appear in any possible second printing, second edition, or translation of the book. It is clear that more than adequate distribution has already been given for the purpose of scholarly study of the book.*

2. It is important that the withdrawal of the imprimi potest *and the reasons for it be communicated both to Father McNeill and to the publisher of the book lest a situation develop again in which the fact that preparations had advanced so far might prompt local authorities to concede a further printing (edition or translation) with ecclesiastical approval.*

3. It seems urgent that Father McNeill be prohibited from any further appearance or lecture on the question of homosexuality and sexual ethics, or in promotion of the book.

Response to the Vatican Letter

The letter begins with a downright falsehood: *In his own words the author presents an "advocacy theology."* In my own words, in the preface to the first edition of *The Church and the Homosexual*, I mention that my critics had accused me of advocacy theology, but I deny that it is the case. I understood "advocacy theology" to be a biased and one-sided presentation of arguments, and I remark in the preface that practically everything ever written on homosexuality, especially every statement from Rome, has been unquestionably advocacy theology. I state, "For my part, I did my best to present fairly all the evidence for and against each thesis I dealt with. I never deliberately omitted or distorted any evidence, even though it was contrary to my convictions."[2] I cannot say the same for the Congregation.

The Congregation's argument for removing the *imprimi potest* implies that I deliberately deceived my Provincial Eamon Taylor and used Machiavellian means to get him to grant the *imprimi potest*. Yet my manuscript was under censorship for a period of over four years. It was first submitted to a committee of six American scholars, both moral theologians and scriptural scholars. That commission included, among others, such eminent theologians as Avery Dulles, Richard McCormick, Robert Springer, and Charles Curran. These censors agreed unanimously that I should be allowed to publish this book. The book was then submitted to another commission of censors in Rome and they too, agreed that it should be published. They did agree that there should be a public debate on the issues I raised.

While it is true that Father Taylor mentioned as one of his reasons for granting an *imprimi potest* that the book should be evaluated by my peers, there never was an understanding that I should somehow limit its distribution to the two dozen moral theologians in America. If that were the only intent for publication, I would have submitted an article to a professional journal, as I did several years previously with my articles on "The Catholic Male Homosexual" in the *Homiletic and Pastoral Review*.

It would have been absurd to publish a book with a major publishing house with the idea of limiting its readership. Both Father Taylor and I thought that my book, because of its nature as a scholarly work, would not appeal to a large reading audience. Consequently, both of us were surprised when it became a best-seller and was translated and published in Danish, French, Spanish, and Italian.

I had been clear from the beginning both with Father Taylor and my peers that I thought no serious advance in moral thought concerning homosexuality could occur without dialogue with those who are living out that orientation and experiencing what the Holy Spirit says to them through their experience. To this day, it seems to me that the essential difference between the Vatican and me has to do with their total distrust in the ability of the Holy Spirit to guide human conscience from within.

Consequently, when I was invited to appear on various talk

shows, such as "The Phil Donahue Show," I welcomed the opportunity, and it was in no way in conflict with the agreement I had made with my superiors.

I feel sure that Father Taylor, when he wrote those words about my peers in the letter granting the *imprimi potest* was sure that my book would receive severely critical and negative reviews from other moral theologians; but such did not prove to be the case. On the contrary, most reviews were very favorable and welcomed my book as a breath of fresh air. Father Taylor was so perplexed by that that at one point about one year after the publication of the book he telephoned me and asked if I myself could somehow arrange to have some more critical reviews published.

The letter also accuses me of "the gravest sort of disregard for the mature study of and loyal support of the authentic magisterium of the church" because my book was published a few days after the publication of *Persona humana*, a document dealing with sexual ethics in general and homosexuality in particular. The letter again fails to mention that on pages 11 to 16 in *The Church and the Homosexual* I do discuss that document, which I refer to in my text as "The Declaration on Certain Questions Concerning Sexual Ethics." But since the document was merely a restatement of the classical condemnation of homosexuality based on a homophobic reading of Scripture and so-called natural law and there was no new argument or position that I had not already fully treated in the text of my book, there was no need to discuss it at greater length.

Finally, the Congregation quotes a press release by then Archbishop Bernardin of Cincinnati (now Cardinal of Chicago). During the year of my visit to Cincinnati, 1977, Archbishop Bernardin was the elected president of the Conference of Catholic Bishops in the United States. The Congregation's letter omits the reason for my presence in Cincinnati: I had been invited by the theology department of Xavier University, a Jesuit-run university, to give a talk on the theology of homosexuality. It was the first time that I encountered a large group of right-wing protesters; they surrounded the hall with placards denouncing the sin of sodomy. I had my audience join in on a decade of the rosary with them to make the point that Mary was not necessarily on their side.

While I was in Cincinnati the local chapter of Dignity held

a banquet in my honor and gave me an award. They invited the Archbishop to be present, but in a letter of response to their invitation he acknowledged that he had not read my book but if the report in the September 20, 1976, *Time* magazine article were accurate, he could not in conscience attend the banquet in my honor. As I was leaving town, reporters read me Archbishop Bernardin's statement. I informed them that I had never suggested that the church had changed or was about to change its teaching on homosexuality. Rather, my public position was that the church *ought* to change its position since it was destructive to the health and happiness of hundreds of thousands of people. Once again, I was falsely accused of trying to deliberately deceive my audiences.

It should be obvious from this series of events that the Congregation felt it was losing the argument and, therefore, fell back on asserting its authority and trying to silence any debate. I decided to obey the orders of the Congregation; the *imprimi potest* was removed from consequent editions of *The Church and the Homosexual*, and I did not speak publicly on the issue of homosexuality for the next nine years. The events that led to my decision to speak out once more are related in chapter 5.

A P P E N D I X   3

The AUTHORITARIAN PERSONALITY

Undoubtedly there is no greater threat to freedom of conscience than that which comes from the authoritarian personality. A close look at the documents emanating from the Vatican reveal, I believe, that the authoritarian personality is alive and well in Rome. German theologian Dr. Norbert Mette calls our attention to the fact that the Church hierarchy has done everything in its power to prevent an interdisciplinary discussion between theology and psychology.[1] What is really at issue here, Mette notes, is the "question of power in the church." The church feels threatened by the radical explanation given by psychology of the origins of domination and power as they appear in any social context including that of the church.

Psychotherapists strive to give awareness and strength to the self. in the face of any extrinsic effort to dominate it and take charge of it. "From such a perspective psychology undeniably provides stimuli which must seem dangerous, if not threatening, to a church which so far has found it difficult to acknowledge the freedom of Christians."[2]

In his classic work, *Escape From Freedom*, Eric Fromm makes the point that in contrast to the Promethean personality who seeks to free him or herself from all dependencies, the authoritarian personality fears freedom and spontaneity and gladly surrenders freedom for security.[3] A primary mechanism of escape from freedom is surrendering one's independence and fusing oneself with something external in order to acquire the strength one feels one lacks. This is most commonly found in strivings for submission or domination, the normal counterparts of neurotic sadomasochism. The masochist often shows a marked dependence on powers outside himself—other people, institutions, even nature or God.

The connection between such masochistic propensities and the authoritarian personality were noted by S. L. Charmé in his article *Religion and the Theory of Masochism*:

> *The masochist is willing to sacrifice all individual decisions, responsibility, or interests and to find meaning, direction, and protection by submitting to some larger power. He identifies with a person, group, cause, nation, or religion which defines the meaning of his life and offers the prestige and strength he lacks as an individual. This form of masochism is associated with authoritarian personalities found both in fascism and religious movements. The appeal of many religious "cults" is based on a similar process. In most cases the cult member willingly sacrifices all signs of individuality in thought and personality in exchange for the security and power offered by the group in general and the leader in particular.[4]*

Fromm observes that the feature common to all authoritarian thinking is the conviction that life is determined by forces outside of one's self or one's interests and wishes. The only possible happiness lies in the submission to those forces. The powerlessness of the human is the leitmotif of masochistic philosophy: "To suffer without complaining is his highest virtue—not the courage of trying to end suffering or at least diminish it. Not to change fate, but to submit to it, is the heroism of the authoritarian character."[5] It is interesting to note that the

Pope ends his recent encyclical *Veritatis Splendor* with a chapter in praise of martyrdom.[6]

As William Meissner observes, sadistic tendencies may be found hand-in-hand with masochistic ones, often in the same personality.[7] They involve wishes to make others dependent on oneself, to have absolute power over others, to rule others in a way that exploits and uses them, to see or make others suffer. These tendencies are usually less conscious and are often covered over by reaction formations and rationalizations of excessive concern for and goodness toward others. "I rule you because I know what is best for you." This is frequently the tone the Church takes toward gay people.

In their massive study culminating in the book, *The Authoritarian Personality*, T. W. Adorno *et al.* uncovered a consistent profile of personality characteristics.[8] Authoritarian individuals tended to adhere rigidly to conventional and generally accepted values; they tended to be uncritically submissive to whatever moral authorities existed in the group to which they belong, authorities whom they frequently idealized; they tended to turn their aggression against anyone violating or rejecting the values they espoused, so that their attitude was often harsh, condemnatory, and punitive; they tended to be tough-minded rather than tender-minded; so that they usually rejected the subjective or imaginative approach to things; their thinking tended to superstition and stereotypes, often in the form of belief in more or less mystical determinants of individual fate and a tendency to think in rigid categories; they were frequently preoccupied with power and control, emphasized issues of power and submission in regard to authority, and identified with powerful figures; their attitude was often hostile, cynical, and paranoid, tending to view the world as dangerous and threatening and projecting strong negative emotions to the outside; and finally sexual fantasies were a source of excessive concern.

The primary effective way to respond to exaggerations of authoritarianism in the Church is to develop the capacity to discern spirits and the spiritual skills required for the exercise of freedom of conscience.

NOTES

Preface

1. All biblical texts are from *The New Jerusalem Bible: Reader's Edition* (New York: Doubleday, 1990) unless otherwise noted.

Part 1. Introduction: The Gay Spiritual Journey

1. Cf. "Letter to the Bishops of the Catholic Church on the Pastoral Care of Homosexual Persons," issued by Cardinal Ratzinger, Prefect for the Congregation for the Defense of the Faith on October 31, 1986. *Readings in Moral Theology No. 8: Dialogue About Catholic Sexual Teaching*, ed. Charles E. Curran and Richard A. McCormick, S.J. (New York: Paulist Press, 1993), pp. 297–308.

2. Will Roscoe, "Living the Tradition: Gay American Indians," *Gay Spirit: Myth and Meaning*, ed. Mark Thompson (New York: St. Martin's Press, 1988).

3. John Boswell, *Christianity, Social Tolerance, and Homosexuality: Gay People in Western Europe from the Beginning of the Christian Era to the Fourteenth Century* (Chicago: University of Chicago Press, 1980).

Chapter 1: Freedom of Conscience and Gay Maturity

1. Gustavo Gutierrez, *We Drink from Our Own Wells: The Spiritual Journey of a People*, trans. Matthew J. O'Connell (New York: Orbis Press, 1984), p. xiv.

2. D. W. Winnicott, *The Maturational Process and the Facilitating Environment: Studies in the Theory of Emotional Development* (New York: International Universities Press, 1965), p. 104.

3. John McNeill, *The Blondelian Synthesis* (Leiden, Holland: E. J. Brill, 1966), pp. 182–83. Cf. appendix 1 for a summary of the philosophy of freedom of the French Catholic philosopher Maurice Blondel. The insights of Blondel into freedom and subjectivity play a major role in this book.

Chapter 2: Freedom of Conscience and the Catholic Church

1. "Pastoral Constitution on the Church in the Modern World," *The Documents of Vatican II*, ed. Walter M. Abbott, S.J. (New York: America Press, 1966), p. 213.

2. Pope John Paul II, *The Splendor of Truth*, chap. I, sec. 27. *Inside the Vatican*, special supplement, November 1993, p. 11.

3. Bishop Francis Murphy, "Let's Start Over: A Bishop Appraises the Pastoral on Women," *Commonweal*, 25 September 1992, pp. 11–15.

4. Ibid.

5. Ibid.

6. "The Role of the Church in the Modern World," *Documents of Vatican II*, p. 244.

7. Vaclav Havel, "The End of the Modern Era," *New York Times*, 1 March 1992, op. ed.

8. Sally Cunneen, *Mother Church: What the Experience of Women Is Teaching Her* (New York: Paulist Press, 1991), pp. 409–10. Cf. also "Mother Church," *America*, 30 November 1991.

9. Cunneen, *Mother Church*, p. 410.

Chapter 3: Discernment of Spirits

1. Murphy, "Let's Start Over," p. 14.

2. William Meissner, *Ignatius of Loyola: The Psychology of a Saint* (New Haven: Yale University Press, 1993), p. 232.

3. David L. Fleming, S.J., *The Spiritual Exercises of St. Ignatius: A Literal Translation and a Contemporary Reading* (St. Louis: The Institute of Jesuit Resources, 1978).

4. Ibid., pp. 206–7.

5. A direct translation from the Hebrew by Phyllis Trible, Professor of Old Testament Studies, Union Theological Seminary, New York, New York. The biblical text is Genesis 2:18.

6. Thomas Gertler, S.J., "East Germany: A Spiritual Discernment," *America*, 30 November 1991, pp. 84–88.

7. Gertler, "East Germany," p. 85.

8. Ibid., p. 86.

9. Ibid., p. 88.

10. Fleming, *Spiritual Exercises*, pp. 212–13.

11. Gertler, "East Germany," p. 87.

12. Ibid.

13. Dietrich Bonhoeffer, *Letters and Papers from Prison* (New York: The Macmillan Company, 1953), p. 84.

14. Gertler, "East Germany," p. 88.

15. Ibid.

Chapter 5: My Personal Experience of Discernment

1. Fleming, *Spiritual Exercises*, "Three Kinds of Humility," pp. 100–102.

2. Ibid., p. 101.

3. Ibid.

4. Ibid.

5. Ibid., p. 103.

6. Ibid., p. 89.

7. Ibid., p. 101.

8. Geske Namgyal Wangchen, *Awakening the Mind of Enlightenment: Meditations on the Buddhist Path* (Boston: Wisdom Publications, 1987), chaps. 10–11 concern the Bodhisattva path.

9. Anthony Perkins, *New York Times*, Obituary, 14 September 1992.

10. Edward Schillebeeckx, *Ministry: Leadership in the Community of Jesus Christ* (New York: Crossroad, 1981), pp. 106–7.

Part 2. Introduction: The Gay Self and the Catholic Hierarchy

1. Congregation for the Doctrine of the Faith, *Letter to the Bishops of the Catholic Church*, "Some Considerations Concerning the Catholic Response to Legislative Proposals on the Non-Discrimination of Homosexual Persons," June 1992.

2. Ibid., pp. 4–5.

3. Congregation for the Doctrine of the Faith, "Letter to the Bishops of the Catholic Church on the Pastoral Care of Homosexual Persons," *Readings in Moral Theology, No. 8: Dialogue About Catholic Sexual Teaching* (New York: Paulist Press, 1993), pp. 287–308.

4. Ibid., p. 302.

5. Richard A. Isay, *Being Homosexual: Gay Men and Their Development* (New York: Farrar, Straus, and Giroux, 1989). This quotation is from the *New York Times*, 2 September 1992.

6. Gilbert Herdt and Andrew Boxer, *Children of Horizons: How Gay and Lesbian Teens Are Leading the Way Out of the Closet* (Boston: Beacon Press, 1993), p. 120.

7. Richard Isay, in a letter to the *New York Times*, 2 September 1992.

8. "Some Considerations Concerning the Catholic Response to Legislative Proposals," p. 2.

9. Ibid., Applications item 14, p. 3, para. 14.

10. *Documents of Vatican II*, "Decree on the Apostolate of the Laity," pp. 489–525.

Chapter 6: Creating the Authentic Gay Self:
The Three-Stage Process

1. Evelyn and James Whitehead, *Seasons of Strength: New Visions of Adult Christian Maturing* (Garden City, New York: Image Books/ Doubleday, 1986), chap. 4: "Passages in Homosexual Holiness."

2. Ibid., p. 54.

3. John Fortunato, *Embracing the Exile: Healing Journeys of Gay Christians* (San Francisco: Harper & Row, 1987), pp. 68–95.

4. Elizabeth Kübler-Ross, *On Death and Dying* (New York: Jason Aronson, 1978).

5. Fortunato, *Embracing the Exile*, p. 91.

6. Whiteheads, *Seasons of Strength*, p. 132.

7. Cf. the explanation of Blondel's category "the necessary and impossible" in chap. 11, pp. 121–26.

8. Winnicott, *Maturational Process*, p. 104.

9. Whiteheads, *Seasons of Strength*, pp. 135–36.

10. Ibid., p. 138.

11. *The Book of Wisdom* along with *Ecclesiasticus* belongs to those Old Testament books referred to as the Apocrypha. They are omitted from some editions of the Bible, but are included in *The New Jerusalem Bible* as deuterocanonical books.

12. *The Boys in the Band* was a movie made in the sixties, portraying the internalized self-hatred of gay men.

13. Herdt and Boxer, *Children of Horizons*. These authors hold the optimistic position that in twenty years or so, ". . . the coming-out process will no longer be necessary, at least in urban cultures" (p. 253).

14. Whiteheads, *Seasons of Strength*, p. 137.

Chapter 7: The Second Passage into Intimacy with Another

1. Whiteheads, *Seasons of Strength*, p. 138.

2. Isay, *Being Homosexual*, p. 148.

3. Kirkridge, an ecumenical retreat center in the Poconos in Pennsylvania, has held gay and Christian retreats annually for the past nineteen years.

4. Thomas E. Clarke, S.J., *Tracing the Spirit: Communities, Social Action, and Theological Reflection*, ed. James E. Hug (Mahwey, N.J.: Paulist Press, 1983), pp. 18–50.

5. Whiteheads, *Seasons of Strength*, pp. 140–41.

Chapter 8: A Public Passage

1. Whiteheads, *Seasons of Strength*, p. 138.

2. *A Challenge to Love: Gay and Lesbian Catholics in the Church*, ed. Robert Nugent (New York: Crossroad, 1983), p. 61.

3. Whiteheads, *Seasons of Strength*, p. 142.

4. Bishop Otis Charles, *Bay Windows* 2:41 (7–13 October 1993).

Chapter 9: Coming Out through a Public Rite of Covenanted Union

1. Kenneth Forman, *From This Day Forward* (Richmond, Va.: Outlook Publishers, 1950), p. 10. I wish to acknowledge my debt of gratitude to Sean Murray for sharing with me his unpublished manuscript, "In Front of God and Everybody: A Gay Man's Guide to Ceremonies of Covenantal Union," 1 April 1992.

2. See n. 5 to chap. 3.

3. Pope Pius XI, *Casti Connubii, The Church and the Reconstruction of the Modern World*, The Social Encyclicals of Pius XI, ed. Terence P. McLaughlin (Garden City, N.Y.: Doubleday, 1957), p. 59. The same point is made strongly in the "Pastoral Constitution on the Church in the Modern World," *Documents of Vatican II*, pp. 314–15: "Therefore, marriage persists as a whole manner and communion of life, and maintains its value and indissolubility, even when offspring are lacking—despite, rather often, the very intense desire of the couple." No. 50.

4. Daniel Maguire, "The Morality of Homosexual Marriage," in Nugent, ed., *A Challenge to Love*, p. 120.

5. John Boswell, *Same-Sex Unions in Pre-Modern Europe*. This manuscript is expected to be published in the spring of 1994.

6. Ibid.

7. Whiteheads, *Seasons of Strength*, p. 186.

Part 3. Introduction: A Means of Liberation for Lesbians and Gay Men

1. Bill Wilson, *As Bill Sees It: Selected Writings of A.A.'s Co-Founder* (New York: Alcoholics Anonymous World Services, Inc., 1976), p. 10.

2. Al Anon is an organization for the family and friends of alcoholics that makes use of the twelve-step program.

3. Gerald May, *Addiction and Grace: Love and Spirituality in the Healing of Addictions* (San Francisco: Harper & Row, 1988), p. 113.

Chapter 10: Intimacy with God

1. Henry Guntrip, *Schizoid Phenomena, Object Relations and the Self* (New York: International Universities Press, 1969).

2. Collect in the Roman Catholic Liturgy for the Second Sunday in Advent.

3. Sebastian Moore, *Jesus: The Liberator of Desire* (New York: Crossroad, 1989), p. 91.

4. *Twelve Steps and Twelve Traditions* (New York: Alcoholics Anonymous World Services, Inc., 1969), p. 21.

5. John J. McNeill, *The Blondelian Synthesis: A Study of the Influence of German Philosophical Sources on the Formation of Blondel's Method and Thought*, vol. 1 in the series *Studies in the History of Christian Thought*, ed. Heiko Oberman *et al.* (Leiden: E. J. Brill, 1966), p. 298.

6. Havel, "End of the Modern Era."

7. Hans Kung, *Does God Exist? An Answer for Today*, trans. Edward Quinn (Garden City, New York: Doubleday, 1980). See "Fundamental Mistrust or Fundamental Trust," pp. 442–47.

8. Matthew Fox, "The Special Journey of the Homosexual . . . and Just About Everybody Else," in *A Challenge to Love: Gay and Lesbian Catholics in the Church*, ed. Robert Nugent (New York: Crossroad, 1987), pp. 189–204.

9. Henri Nouwen, *Life of the Beloved: Spiritual Living in a Secular World* (New York: Crossroad, 1992), p. 28.

10. Gerald May, *Addiction and Grace*, see pp. 149–89.

11. McNeill, *Blondelian Synthesis*, see pp. 232–33 for Blondel's concept of privation.

12. Paul Tillich, *The Eternal Now* (New York: Charles Scribner's Sons, 1963), pp. 173–85.

13. Havel, "End of the Modern Era."

14. John Carmody, *A Theology of Illness*, The Warren Lecture Series in Catholic Studies, University of Tulsa, 1993.

15. May, *Addiction and Grace*, pp. 178–81. Cf. also Gerald May, *The Awakened Heart: Living Beyond Addiction* (San Francisco: Harper, 1991), pp. 93–110.

16. Eric Fromm, *Escape from Freedom* (New York: Avon Books, 1965).

17. The Jewish toast "le chaim" is derived from the biblical text, "I put before you life and death. Choose life!"

18. McNeill, *Blondelian Synthesis*, see "The Necessary and the Impossible," pp. 148–49.

19. Maurice Blondel, *L'Action: Essai d'une critique de la vie et d'une science de la pratique* (Paris: Felix Alain, 1893), p. 321.

20. Ibid., p. 354.

21. Ibid., p. 461.

Chapter 11: Opening a Dialogue between the Feminist and the Masculine Understandings of Twelve-Step Spirituality

1. Gail Unterberger, "Twelve Steps for Women Alcoholics," *The Christian Century*, 9 December 1989, pp. 1150–52.

2. *Twelve Steps and Twelve Traditions*, p. 136.

3. Ibid., p. 133.

4. Ibid., p. 184.

5. Ibid., p. 188.

6. Unterberger, "Twelve Steps for Women," p. 1151.

7. Elizabeth Johnson, *She Who Is: The Mystery of God in Feminist Theological Discourse* (New York: Crossroad, 1992), pp. 62–65. See also Johnson, "A Theological Case for God-She: Expanding the Treasury of Metaphors," *Commonweal*, 29 January 1993, pp. 9–14.

8. Ibid.

9. Joseph Campbell, *The Hero's Journey* (San Francisco: Harper & Row, 1990).

10. Jean Fitzpatrick, *A Year of Sobering Thoughts*, vol. 4 (March 1979–March 1980).

11. *Twelve Steps and Twelve Traditions*, Step 5, p. 56; Step 12, p. 109.

12. Unterberger, "Twelve Steps for Women," p. 1151.

13. Ibid.

14. Linda Schierse Leonard, *Witness to the Fire: Creativity & the Veil of Addiction* (Boston: Shambhala, 1990), p. xii.

15. McNeill, *Blondelian Synthesis*, see "Methodology of Immanence," pp. 16–17, 26–33, 60–62; "God as Immanent," pp. 182–83.

16. Martin Buber, *Eclipse of God: Studies in the Relation between Religion and Philosophy* (New York: Harper & Row, 1952), p. 7.

17. Carter Heyward, *The Redemption of God: A Theology of Mutual Relationships* (Lanham, Md.: University Press of America, 1982).

18. Blondel, *L'Action*, p. 442.

19. Ibid., p. 443.

20. Ibid., p. 441.

21. Ibid., p. 446.

Part 4. Introduction: Homosexuality and the New Testament

1. Gary David Comstock, *Gay Theology without Apology* (Cleveland: The Pilgrim Press, 1993), pp. 38–48.

2. Boswell, *Christianity, Social Tolerance, and Homosexuality*, pp. 91–117.

3. Comstock, *Gay Theology*, p. 39.

4. J. Edgar Brun, "Old Testament History and the Development of a Sexual Ethic," *The New Morality* (Philadelphia: Westminster).

5. John J. McNeill, *The Church and the Homosexual*, 4th ed. (Boston: Beacon Press, 1993), pp. 42–67.

6. My primary source for this section on the Gay Centurion is an unpublished manuscript by a Franciscan biblical scholar, entitled "Wrestling with the Spirit in a Living Tradition," who requested to remain unnamed at this time. Cf. also Donald Mader, "The *Entimos Pais* of Matthew 8:5–13 and Luke 7:1–10," *Paidika* 1:1 (1989): 27–37.

7. H. M. D. Parker, *The Roman Legions* (Cambridge: W. Holder, 1958).

8. W. W. Buckland, *The Roman Law of Slavery: The Condition of the Slave in Private Law from Augustus to Justinian* (New York: AMS Press, 1969).

9. "Wrestling with the Spirit in a Living Tradition," p. 28.

10. Buckland, *Roman Law*, pp. 36–37.

11. I wish to thank Nancy Wilson, an elder of Metropolitan Community Church, for this insight into Jesus' family of choice.

Chapter 12: God's Love of Gays

1. Nouwen, *Life of the Beloved*.

2. Moore, *Jesus: The Liberator of Desire*, see "The Crisis of an Ethic Without Desire: Human Sexuality," pp. 89–107.

3. Nouwen, *Life of the Beloved*, p. 27.

4. Johnson, *She Who Is*, pp. 9–14.

5. Buber, *Eclipse of God*, pp. 13–46.

6. Hans Loewald, *Psychoanalysis and the History of the Individual* (New Haven: Yale University Press, 1978).

7. Heinz Kohut, *How Does Analysis Cure?* (Chicago: The University of Chicago Press, 1994), pp. 69–79.

8. Nouwen, *Life of the Beloved*, p. 30–31.

Chapter 13: The Special Nature of the Gay and Lesbian Love of God

1. Patrick Arnold, *Wildmen, Warriors and Kings: Masculine Spirituality in the Bible* (New York: Crossroad, 1991), pp. 172–73.

2. *The Confessions of Saint Augustine*.

3. Samuel Menashe, *Collected Poems* (Orono, Maine: National Poetry Foundation, University of Maine, 1986).

Epilogue: Emerging from the Heart of the World

1. Jacques Perotti, *Les Exclus de l'Église: Apprendre à s'Aimer* (Paris: Editions Filipacchi, 1993).

2. Richard Tarnas, *The Passion of the Western Mind: Understanding the Ideas that Have Shaped Our World View* (New York: Ballantine Books, 1991).

3. Ibid., p. 492 n. 9.

4. Ibid.

5. Ibid., pp. 423–24.

6. Ibid., p. 426.

7. Ibid., p. 429.

8. Meissner, *Ignatius of Loyola*, pp. 230–40.

9. Ibid., p. 363.

10. Tarnas, *Passion of the Western Mind*, p. 493 n. 10.

11. G. W. F. Hegel, *Phenomenology of Spirit* (Oxford: Oxford University Press, 1977), p. 248.

12. Tarnas, *Passion of the Western Mind*, p. 442.

13. Robert Bellah, *Habits of the Heart* (New York: Harper & Row, 1988).

14. The list which follows of evidences of the feminine ar-

chetype development in the world today can be found in Tarnas, *Passion of the Western Mind*, pp. 442–43.

15. Ibid., pp. 443–44.

16. Carl Jung, *Memories, Dreams, Reflections* (New York: Pantheon, 1973), p. 234.

17. Tarnas, *Passion of the Western Mind*, p. 444.

18. Constance Fitzgerald, O.C.D., "Impasse and Dark Night," in *Women's Spirituality: Resources for Christian Development*, ed. Joann Wolski Conn (New York: Paulist Press, 1986), p. 290.

19. Tarnas, *Passion of the Western Mind*, p. 445.

20. Judy Grahn, *Blood, Bread, and Roses: How Menstruation Created the World* (Boston: Beacon Press, 1993), pp. 276–78.

21. G. Rattray Taylor, *Sex in History* (New York: Vanguard Press, 1954), pp. 72*ff.*

22. Mary Hunt, "Get a Life: A Feminist Theological Perspective on Death," a talk given at the Gay and Lesbian Conference at Kirkridge Retreat Center, June 1993. See also Rosemary Radford Ruether, *Sexism and God-Talk* (Boston: Beacon Press, 1983), p. 257.

23. Blondel's concept of "the necessary and the impossible" is developed in chap. 10, "Intimacy with God."

24. Pierre Teilhard de Chardin, *The Future of Man* (New York: Harper & Row, 1964), p. 302 n. 1.

25. Wolfgang Harthauser, "Der Massenmord an Homosexuellen im Dritten Reich," in *Der Grosse Tabu*, ed. William S. Schlegel (Munich: Rutten & Leening Verlag, 1967), pp. 17–37.

26. Ibid.

27. Louis Crompton, "Gay Genocide: From Leviticus to Hitler," *Salvatorian Justice and Peace Commission: Gay Minority Task Force.*

28. C. G. Jung, *The Collected Works*, No. 9, Pt. 1, *The Archetypes and the Collective Unconscious*, 2d ed., ed. Gerhard Adler *et al.*, trans. R. F. C. Hull (Princeton, N.J.: Princeton University Press, 1968), pp. 86–87.

29. Mary Hunt, *Fierce Tenderness: A Feminist Theology of Friendship* (New York: Crossroad, 1990).

30. Pierre-Claude Nappey, "An Open Letter on Homosexuality," *Sex: Thoughts for Contemporary Christians*, ed. Michael Taylor (Garden City, N.Y.: Doubleday, 1972), p. 211.

31. Ibid., pp. 217–18.

32. Elinor Yaknes, *New York Times*, 25 February 1972, p. 41.

33. Richard D. Mohr, *Gay Ideas: Outing and Other Controversies* (Boston: Beacon Press, 1992), pp. 140–44.

34. Nappey, "Open Letter," p. 210.

35. J. Edgar Brun, "Old Testament History and the Development of Sexual Ethics," *The New Morality* (Philadelphia: Westminster Press).

36. Nappey, "Open Letter," p. 217.

37. Ibid., p. 218.

38. Eugene Kennedy, *The New Sexuality: Myths, Fables and Hang-Ups* (Garden City, N.Y.: Doubleday, 1973), p. 179.

39. Rainer Maria Rilke, *Letters to a Young Poet*, trans. M. D. Herter (New York: Pantheon, 1959), pp. 58–59.

40. Ibid., p. 86.

41. Ibid.

42. Ibid., p. 87.

43. Jung, *Archetypes and the Collective Unconscious*, pp. 86–87.

44. Matthew Kelty, *Flute Solo: Reflections of a Trappist Hermit* (Garden City, N.Y.: Doubleday, 1980), p. 45.

Appendix 1: Maurice Blondel: The Philosopher of Freedom

1. The primary source for this appendix is Maurice Blondel's *L'Action: Essai d'une critique de la vie et d'une science de la pratique* (Paris: Felix Alain, 1893). Cf. also *Les premier écrits de Maurice Blondel II* (Paris: 1956).

My primary work on Blondel is *The Blondelian Synthesis: A Study of the Influence of German Philosophical Sources on the Formation of Blondel's Method and Thought*, vol. 1 in the series *Studies in the History of Christian Thought*, ed. Heiko Oberman *et al.* (Leiden, Holland: E. J. Brill, 1966). I have developed Blondel's philosophy of freedom and moral life in "Necessary Structures of Freedom," *Proceedings: Jesuit Philosophical Association* (1968); "Freedom of Conscience in Theological Perspective," *Conscience: Its Freedom and Limitations*, ed. William C. Bier (New York: Pastoral Psychology Series, Fordham University Press, 1971).

The best English language commentary is James M. Somerville's *Total Commitment: Blondel's L'Action* (Washington, D.C.: Corpus Books, 1968).

2. McNeill, *Blondelian Synthesis*, p. 66.

3. Blondel, *L'Action*, p. vii.

4. Ibid.

5. Ibid., "Methodology of Immanence," pp. 16–17, 23–33.

6. Ibid., p. 298.

7. Ibid., "Privation," pp. 232–33.

8. Ibid., "Necessary Logic of Freedom," pp. 200–201.

9. Maurice Blondel, "Illusion Idealist," *Les Premier Écrits de Maurice Blondel*, Vol. 2, *Bibliothèque de Philosophie Contemporaine* (Paris: Universitaires de France, 1956), pp. 110–11.

10. Blondel, *L'Action*, p. vii.

11. Blondel, *L'Action*, "Option for the Transcendent," pp. 182–83.

12. Ibid., "Final Option," p. 100.

13. Pedro Arrupé, S.J. "Reflections on Death," *America* (16 February 1991): 164.

14. Blondel, *L'Action*, p. 492.

Appendix 2: The Church and the Homosexual:
Its Condemnation and My Response

1. *Readings in Moral Theology, No. 8: Dialogue about Catholic Sexual Teaching*, ed. Charles E. Curran and Richard A. McCormick, S.J. (New York: Paulist Press, 1993). This collection reproduces in full the letter sent in the summer of 1978 from the Congregation for the Doctrine of the Faith to the Jesuit Superior General, Pedro Arrupé, S.J., regarding *The Church and the Homosexual*.

2. McNeill, *Church and the Homosexual*, p. 24.

Appendix 3: The Authoritarian Personality

1. Norbert Mette, "Psychology Instead of Theology?" *Concilium* 1991/6 XVI.

2. Ibid., XV.

3. Fromm, *Escape from Freedom* (New York: Avon Books, 1965).

4. S. L. Charmé, "Religion and the Theory of Masochism," *Journal of Religion and Health* 22 (1983): 221–33.

5. Fromm, *Escape from Freedom*, pp. 194–95.

6. Pope John Paul II, "The Splendor of Truth," *Inside the Vatican* (November 1993).

7. Meissner, *Ignatius of Loyola*, pp. 232, 262.

8. T. W. Adorno *et al.*, *The Authoritarian Personality* (New York: Harper, 1950).